Develop the Territory under Your Hat—THINK!

Critical Thinking:
A Workout For A Stronger Mind

Dr. Natacha Billups-Thomas

Order this book online at www.trafford.com
or email orders@trafford.com

Most Trafford titles are also available at major online book retailers.

Printed in the United States of America.

ISBN: 978-1-4269-8945-2 (sc)
ISBN: 978-1-4269-8946-9 (e)

Trafford rev. 01/09/2012

 www.trafford.com

North America & international
toll-free: 1 888 232 4444 (USA & Canada)
phone: 250 383 6864 ♦ fax: 812 355 4082

*First off, I would like to thank the Creator
for his Amazing Grace and Mercy.*

*I dedicate this book to my husband Tim, children
Najuwan and Nylah, parents Delores and Woodrow
Billups, Jr., brother and sister-in-law Woodrow
and Monique Billups, III, nephew Josiah Billups,
mother-in-law Mabel Thomas, aunts, uncles, cousins.
Without you, my loving, nurturing and supportive family,
this journey, this book would not have been possible.*

ACKNOWLEDGEMENTS

My deepest thanks go to my family. Najuwan, because of you, mommie realizes the importance of not giving up and continues to strive forward. My parents, Delores and Woodrow A. Billups, Jr., brother Woodrow A. Billups III, grandmother, Virginia Maynor, aunts, uncles, cousins, I thank you for stepping in being a surrogate to Naj, taking him to the park, library (story time), swimming, fishing, visiting other relatives as well as baby-sitting him during my labor of this doctoral degree. And of course, the Divine Creator who always knows exactly what I need, and exactly when I need it.

To my deceased grandparents – Mildred A. Billups, Woodrow A. Billups, Sr., Horace Maynor, and Theodore Richardson for the influential part you played in my life. I love you and thank you!

To my committee members: Dr. Lenneal Henderson, chair; Dr. Lee Mahon, research faculty; Dr. Malcolm Bonner, faculty reader; Obie Clayton, external reader; and Gregory Farngalo, student reader, I sincerely thank you for your encouragement, advice, and support.

CONTENTS

Acknowledgements vi

List Of Tables x

CHAPTER ONE: INTRODUCTION 1
    Overview of the Study 1
    Statement of the Problem 3
    Purpose of the Study 4
    Historical Background 5
    Research Questions 6
    Significance of the Research 6
    Limitations to the Study 8
    Definition of Terms 8
    Introduction 10

CHAPTER TWO: LITERATURE REVIEW 10
    Importance of Critical Thinking and Writing 11
    Methods of Teaching Critical Thinking Skills 12
        Skills Approach 12
        Problem Solving Approach 13
        Logic Approach 15
        Information Processing Approach 15
        Multi-aspect Approach 16
    Definition of Critical Thinking 19
    The Georgia Grade Five Writing Assessment 21
    Philosophy of the Georgia Grade Five Writing Assessment 22
    The Six Stages of Writing 22
        Stage 1: Emerging Writer 23
        Stage 2: Developing Writer 23
        Stage 3: Focusing Writer 23
        Stage 4: Experimenting Writer 23
        Stage 5: Engaging Writer 24
        Stage 6: Extending Writer 24

Beginning to Write 25
    Session One 25
    Session Two 26
Steps of the Writing Process 27
    Pre-writing Step 27
    Drafting Step 29
    Revising and Editing Step 29
    Writing Final Draft and Proofreading 31
Writing Workshop 31
    Mini-lesson 32
    Introducing the Strategy 33
    Demonstrating the Strategy 33
    Practicing the Strategy 33
The Process Writing Classroom 33
Text Structure 34
    Narrative Text 34
    Expository Text 34
Spelling 36
    Analysis of Spelling Errors 36
    Development of Spelling 36
Mechanics of Writing 38
Grammar of the English Language 38
America's Choice Program 38
Research Related to America's Choice School Design 39
History of Appalachia Educational Laboratory (AEL) 40
Summary 41
Introduction 42
Research Design 42

CHAPTER THREE: METHODOLOGY 42
Subjects 43
America's Choice Elementary Instructional Program 46
Instrumentation 47
    Instrumentation 1: Teacher Survey (Quantitative) 47
    Instrumentation 2: Teacher Focus Group (Qualitative) 47
    Instrumentation 3: Student Focus Groups (Qualitative) 48
    Instrumentation 4: Writing Scores of 5th Grade Students
    (Quantitative) 48

CHAPTER FOUR: RESULTS 49
    Introduction... 49
        Analysis of Teacher Survey: 50
      Research Question One... 50
        Analysis of Teacher Focus Group: Questions 1 through 7 57
      Research Question Two.. 57
        Analysis of Teacher Focus Group: Questions 8 through 15..... 60
      Research Question Three.. 64
        Analysis of Student Focus Groups..................................... 65
    Discussion of Findings 72

CHAPTER FIVE: DISCUSSION, SUMMARY, AND
RECOMMENDATIONS 72
      Research Question One... 72
      Research Question Three.. 74
      Research Question Two.. 73
    Summary... 77
    Recommendations.. 78
    Implications 79

References 81
    Appendix A: Teacher Survey... 89
    Appendix B: Teacher Focus Group Questions............................ 92

Appendixes
    Appendix C: Student Focus Group 1 Questions........................ 96
    Appendix D: Student Focus Group 2 Questions......................... 99
    Appendix E: Student Focus Group 2 Questions 102
    Appendix F: Teacher Recruitment Letter 105
    Appendix G: Informed Consent Letter for Teachers 107
    Appendix H: Assent Letter for 5th Grade Students................. 110
    Appendix I: Informed Consent Letter for Parents................... 112

LIST OF TABLES

Table 1.   Elementary School Profile of Student Achievement 25

Table 2.   Ability to Write with Clarity 50

Table 3.   Ability to Write Using Correct Grammar 51

Table 4.   Ability to Write Using Correct Punctuation 51

Table 5.   Ability to Develop a Writing Style 51

Table 6.   Ability to Transmit Information/Knowledge Effectively 52

Table 7.   Ability to Understand What They Read 52

Table 8.   Ability to Move from Instructions and Concepts to
            Execution of Projects Independently 53

Table 9.   Ability to Use General Concepts in Content Areas 53

Table 10.   Ability to Use Appropriate Vocabulary during
            Writing in the Content Areas 54

Table 11.   Rating of Students' Critical Thinking Skills 54

Table 12.   America's Choice Program Benefited Writing Skills 55

Table 13.   America's Choice Program Benefited
            Critical Thinking Skills 55

Table 14.   America's Choice Program Provided Staff
            Development for Teachers 56

Table 15.   America's Choice Program Beneficial to Fifth Graders 56

Table 16.   Interest in America's Choice Curriculum 57

Table 17.   America's Choice Curriculum Training Program 57

Table 18.   Training Personnel 58

Table 19.   Students Experiencing Difficulty in Writing 58

Table 20.   Students Knowledgeable about Thinking Critically 59

Table 21.   Challenge Students to be Critical Thinkers 59

Table 22.   Increased Students' Critical Thinking Ability 60

CHAPTER ONE

INTRODUCTION

Overview of the Study

Chapter one of this study of a selected group of fifth grade student's ability to utilize higher order thinking skills describes a statement of the problem, purpose of the study, historical background, research goals/objectives, and limitations of the study, definition of terms, and significance of the study. As a result of America's Choice program on critical thinking and writing skills, this study will focus on the impact of this program on students' critical thinking and writing skills.

Research on writing by Langer & Applebee (1987) clearly indicated that carefully crafted writing assignments engage higher order thinking skills allowing students to move beyond mere knowledge and comprehension skills to application, analysis, and evaluation (the more cognitively complex skills on Bloom's taxonomy).

Fulwilder and Young (2000) explained in their introduction to Language and Connections: Writing and Reading Across the Curriculum—Write to Communicate that higher order thinking skills were related to students' ability to write. Britton, Martian, McLeod, and Rosen (1975) reported that transactional writing was synonymous with writing to accomplish something, to inform, instruct, or persuade. Writing to learn is different. People write as well as talk with others to convey their perceptions of reality. The primary function of expressive language is not to communicate, but to order and represent experience to our own understanding. In this sense, language provided us with a unique way of knowing and becomes a tool

1

for discovering, for shaping meaning and for reaching understanding (Fulwilder & Young, 2000).

According to Ennis and Norris (1989, p. 4), "Critical thinking is a reflective and reasonable method of thinking that is focused on deciding what to believe in or do" Patrick (1986) indicated that limited definitions focus on evaluation or appraisal. Critical thinking is the "formulation and use of criteria to make warranted judgments about knowledge claims, normative statements, and methods of inquiry, policy decisions, alternative position on public issues, or any other object of concern" (p. 1).

Patrick further found that critical thinking, defined narrowly, is an essential element of general cognitive processes, such as problem solving or decision making, but not synonymous with them. Patrick explained that critical thinking, whether conceived broadly or not implied curiosity, skepticism, reflection, and rationality. Critical thinkers have a propensity to raise and explore questions about beliefs, claims, evidence, definitions, conclusions, and actions.

Patrick (1986) acknowledged that:

> The ability to think critically can free students from fetters or ignorance, confusion, and unjustified claims about ideals and reality. Ability thinking may also contribute to dissatisfaction with tyrants or totalitarian societies and to the improvement of democratic governments and free societies" (p. 2). Strategies and skills in critical thinking are keys to independent and learning, which can be transferred to subjects and objects of inquiry within and outside of school. Patrick (1986) avows that "students can gain enduring intellectual abilities, which can be used long after particular facts have been forgotten." Students are "empowered as learners and as citizens to think and act more effectively" (p. 2).

Patrick (1986) further confirms that all students, regardless of social class or presumed limitations in ambition or ability have some degree of potential to think critically. This potential can be developed to the fullest by embedding critical thinking in the core curriculum, and school subjects required of all students. Students' capabilities to think critically are likely to be increased if they practice strategies and skills systemically and extensively in all subjects in a matter that is consistent wit their development and prior learning experiences.

Furthermore, subject-specific teaching of critical thinking may be the most effective means to develop students' abilities to transfer strategies and skills to similar subjects in school and problems in life outside school. By contrast, separate courses on critical thinking seem to be rather weak means of developing cognitive strategies and skills (Patrick, 1986).

Statement of the Problem

Why are critical thinking and writing skills important for elementary students? As many educators may seem to agree, the information explosion is a reality increasing, both the amount of information and the rate of increase, which is itself increasing (Bloom, 1956). Those who seek knowledge need the ability to rapidly select, comprehend, analyze, and synthesize information (Bloom, 1956).

According to Johnson (1993), writing across the curriculum has been emphasized in the literature since the early 1980s, when the National Assessment of Education Progress found that students writing performance has shown little improvement over that period. Writing to learn emphasizes better thinking. The focus is on development of ideas, leaving mechanics and forms to be dealt with after students have control of content (Pearce, 1983).

Carefully chosen tasks require active involvement of students in connecting and integrating ideas as they write (Emig, 1977; Fulwilder, 1986; Gere, 1985; Tchudi & Huerta, 1983). Frequent participation in write-to-learn activities also helps students improve their writing, even though this may not be the main purpose. Although writing has often been used to assess learning in secondary classrooms, little time has been devoted to write-to-learn activities such as journals or first-draft writing (Applebee, 1981; Britton et al., 1975; Gere, 1985). Langer and Applebee (1987) found that content area writing can be assist learning "in three primary ways: (1) to gain relevant knowledge and experience in preparing for new activities; (2) to review and consolidate what is known or has been learned; and, (3) to reformulate and extend ideas experiences" (p. 136).

Elementary school students are at an ideal age to undertake the process and practice of storing information. The challenge that students face is the absence or prior instruction or exposure to higher order thinking skills. The students at the elementary school selected for this study are not disciplined about developing critical thinking skills in their school subjects. Part of this challenge may be the absence of prior instruction or exposure to higher order thinking skills.

Purpose of the Study

The purpose of this study is two-fold. First, to analyze the effects and impact of using higher order thinking skills in social studies using the America's Choice Writer's Workshop under the America's Choice Program with students at a selected elementary school. The second purpose is to examine students' ability to utilize higher order thinking skills. The premise is that students will be able to use questioning techniques when they are faced with academic tasks.

The emphasis of this study is what has or has not been accomplished by the schools and school systems with the results of identifying and offering lessons and activities which will allow teachers to integrate critical thinking into the curriculum. This research study will provide a plan on what needs to be done in order to implement these techniques into the curriculum. The population to be served by this study will be selected fifth grade students in a selected public school system.

Historical Background

As I reminisce about my years as an educator, preparing my students to think critically was a rigorous task. My mission each year as I obtained a new group of students, was to get them to use questioning techniques, so when they left my classroom, they could take what they had learned and apply it to other academic areas of learning.

"People have been thinking about 'critical thinking' and have been researching how to teach it for about a hundred years. Socrates began this approach to learning over 2,000 years ago" (Fisher, 2001, p. 2). John Dewey, philosopher, psychologist, and educator, 1910-1939 according to Fisher (2001) is widely regarded as the father of modern critical thinking which Dewey called "reflective thinking" (p. 2). Glaser (1961) broadened the term critical thinking to include the examination of statements. One of the most famous contributors to the development of critical thinking was Ennis (1962 to 1979), who gained wide currency in the field. Critical thinking is reasonable, reflective thinking that is focused on deciding what to believe or do (Norris & Ennis, 1989).

Research Questions

The primary research questions that guided this study were organized as follows: Why were critical thinking and writing skills important for elementary school students?

1. Were there differences in teachers' opinions and perceptions regarding the impact of America's Choice Program on fifth grade students' critical thinking and writing skills?
2. Were there differences in teachers' opinions regarding 5th grade students' critical thinking skills as a result of their participation in the America's Choice program?
3. Were there differences in 5th grade students' opinions regarding their writing skills as a result of their participation in the America's Choice program?

Significance of the Research

According to Gough (1991), "Perhaps most importantly in today's information age, thinking skills are viewed as crucial for educated persons to cope with a rapidly changing world. Many educators believe that specific knowledge will not be as important to tomorrow's workers and citizens as the ability to learn and make sense of new information" (p. 1).

Cotton (1988) states, "in the twentieth century, the ability to engage in careful, reflective thought has been viewed in various ways such as a fundamental characteristic of an educated person, as a requirement for responsible citizenship in a democratic society, and, more recently, as an employability skill for an increasingly wide range of jobs" (p. 1). Gough's (1991) words quoted earlier epitomize the existing viewpoint in education about the significance of teaching today's students to think critically and creatively.

According to Cotton (1988), "Virtually all writers on this subject discuss thinking skills in connection with the two related phenomena of modern technology and fast-paced change" (p. 1). Robinson (1987), for example, states in her 1987 practicum report that teaching children to become effective thinkers is increasingly recognized as an immediate goal for education. If students are to function successfully in a highly technical society, then they must be equipped with lifelong learning and thinking skills necessary to acquire and process information in an ever-changing world (p. 16). Beyth-Meron et al. (1987) underscore this point, characterizing thinking skills as means to making good choices such as thinking skills necessary tools in a society characterized by rapid change, many alternatives of action, and numerous individual and collective choices and decisions (p. 216).

As stated by Cotton (1988), the societal factors that create a need for well-developed thinking skills are only part of the story. Educators, employers, and others call for more and better thinking skills instruction in schools in order that young people in America, in general, will exhibit an impressive level of skill in critical or creative thinking.

The following observation from Norris (1985) is typical: "Critical thinking ability is not widespread. Most students generally do not score well on tests that measure students' ability to recognize assumptions, evaluate arguments, and appraise inferences" (p. 44). Likewise, Robinson (1987) noted that "While the importance of cognitive development has become widespread, students' performance on measures of higher-order thinking ability has displayed a critical need for students to develop the skills and attitudes of effective thinking" (p. 13).

There is yet another major force behind the call for improved thinking skills instruction. Educators generally agree that it is in fact possible to increase students' creative and critical thinking capacities through instruction and practice (Robinson, 1987). Ristow (1988) notes that, in the past, these capacities have often been regarded as "a fluke of nature, a genetic predisposition such as qualities that are either possessed or not possessed by their owner and that education can do very little to develop these qualities (p. 44). Ristow goes on to say "However, a great deal of the research currently being reported indicates that the direct teaching of creative skills can produce better, more creative thinkers" (p. 44). Presseisen (1986) makes this point even more forcefully, asserting that "the most basic premise in the current thinking skills movement is the notion that students can learn to think better if schools concentrate on teaching them how to do so" (p. 17).

Limitations to the Study

The study was limited to the investigation of selected fifth grade students attending a selected elementary school. Therefore, the sample size is too small to generalize the results of this study to a similar population of fifth grade students. Another limitation is that teachers' opinions and perceptions about America's Choice program and its impact on students' critical thinking and writing skills may be biased and too opinionated to generalize to teachers of similar populations and circumstances.

Definition of Terms

Bloom's Taxonomy is a popular instructional model developed by the prominent educator Benjamin Bloom. Bloom's Taxonomy categorizes thinking skills from the concrete to the abstract – knowledge, comprehension, application, analysis, synthesis, evaluation, which are considered higher-order skills (Bloom, 1956).

Critical Thinking is reflective and reasonable thinking that is focused on deciding what to believe or do (Ennis & Norris, 1989, p. 4).

Cognition is the mental operations involved in thinking; the biological/neurological processes of the brain that facilitate thought (Alvino, 1990).

Creative Thinking is a novel way of seeing or doing things that is characterized by four components – fluency (generating many ideas), flexibility (shifting perspectives easily), originality (conceiving of something new), and elaboration (building on other ideas) (Alvino, 1990).

Infusion is integrating thinking skills instruction into the regular curriculum; infused programs are commonly contrasted to separate programs, which teach thinking skills as a curriculum (Alvino, 1990).

Metacognition is the process of planning, assessing, and monitoring one's own thinking; the highest level of mental functioning (Alvino, 1990).

Thinking Skills are the set of basic and advance skills and sub skills that govern a person's mental process. These skills consist of knowledge, dispositions, and cognitive and metacognitive operations (Alvino, 1990).

Transfer is the ability to apply thinking skills taught separately to any subject (Alvino, 1990).

Writing process is a recursive pattern of pre-writing, drafting, revision, editing, and publishing (Graves, 1983).

Writing Workshop is an instructional arrangement that is used for students to learn about the writing process and includes a time to write (Calkins, 1986).

CHAPTER TWO

LITERATURE REVIEW

Introduction

The purpose of this research study is to examine students' ability to utilize higher order thinking skills. With the help of selected relevant literature on this issue, key concepts and definitions of writing as critical thinking are discussed. Various aspects of the America's Choice program were discussed with related goals and objectives. Writing, as it relates to critical thinking concepts and the America's Choice program was applied to a study of a Georgia elementary school with the goal to improve the writing capabilities of its students.

Writing has often been used to assess learning in classrooms; however, little time has been devoted to write-to-learn activities. Atwell (1998), Murray (1996), Avery (1993), Graves (1991), Langer and Applebee (1987), Gere (1985), Applebee (1981), and Britton (1975) found that content area critical thinking and writing can be used to assist learning in three primary ways: (1) to gain relevant knowledge and experience in preparing for new activities; (2) to review and consolidate what is known or has been learned; and (3) to reformulate and extend ideas and experiences.

Writing is one of the main ways one has to record his or her learning so he or she can show his or her teacher what he or she has learned. Writing is not a product; writing is a process. Developing one's ideas involves "putting some kind of ideas onto paper or screen so one can see them, return to them, explore them, question them, share them, clarify them, change them, and expand them" (Copley, 1995, p. 2).

Humans were born to think; it is almost impossible to stop people from thinking. Writing helps people to think more carefully and completely. America's Choice Program involves getting students to "think about and to find the words to explain what they learn, how they understand, what they are learning, and what their own process of learning involves" (Copley, 1995, p. 2).

America's Choice is a program initiated by the National Center on Education and the Economy (NCEE) (2001). The primary focus of America's Choice is to provide the tools and technical assistance the nation needs to lead the world in education and training. The America's Choice School Design objective is a comprehensive school reform program that provides schools, school systems and states with the designs, materials and assistance they need to ensure that all students leave high school ready to do rigorous college level work.

America's Choice Program is related to the issue of writing and critical thinking because thinking and writing promotes clarification and organization of ideas and helps develop problem solving and communication skills. Thinking and writing also facilitates interaction between instructor and student because writing is inherently active, not passive (NCEE, 2001).

Importance of Critical Thinking and Writing

Why is critical thinking and writing important for social studies students? As many educators may seem to agree, the information explosion is an increasing reality. Both the amount of information and the rate of increase is itself increasing. Those who seek knowledge need the ability to rapidly select, comprehend, analyze, and synthesize information (Weinstein, 1993).

Elementary school students are at an ideal age to undertake the process and practice of storing information. The challenge student's face is the absence of prior instruction or exposure to higher order thinking skills. The challenge that students face is the absence of prior instruction or exposure to higher order thinking skills. The goal for the students at the selected elementary school as part of the Early Intervention Program is to be able to use questioning techniques when they are faced with academic tasks. To accomplish this, higher order thinking skills were infused with writing using America's Choice Program Writer's Workshop.

Through the Writer's Workshop, students were taught critical thinking skills infused with the writing process in content area classes. Students were assigned research projects in an area of social studies, pose hypotheses with higher level questions, and the teacher will teach the writing process of pre-writing, writing, revising, editing, and publishing.

Today's young people, as adults, will be faced with pressing, global problems that will demand solutions. Educators need to help students develop a vision and the capacity to meet the challenges that will face them. Teachers should encourage and teach students how to question, analyze, generate creative solutions, and work cooperatively. More than ever before, "critical thinking or higher order thinking should be a primary item on the educational agenda" (Court, 1991, p. 1).

Selman (1989) identified five approaches to teaching critical thinking. These are skills approach, problem solving approach, logic approach, information-processing approach, and multi-aspect approach.

Methods of Teaching Critical Thinking Skills

Skills Approach

One of the first methods of teaching critical thinking that has gained widespread popularity is based on the idea that critical thinking can be broken down into lists of discrete, teachable skills or processes. Lists of these are often related to the higher levels of Bloom's Taxonomy (1956). Analyzing, classifying and synthesizing are viewed as critical thinking skills. This approach is appealing because it is "straightforward and manageable" (Selman, 1989, p. 115).

Teachers can design tasks by which students can practice each of these skills. Students might be asked to classify the centuries of the presidents, in the belief that the skill of classifying can then be transferred to other situations, such as classifying arguments. This assumption is false. If critical thinking is viewed as a set of skills, these skills must be assumed to be general skills, applicable in all situations, and this approach is simply not workable. Analysis is a vastly different thing in different situations. Analyzing "an argument, poem, political situation, chemical compound, or algebra problem require different knowledge and abilities" (Selman, 1989, p. 115).

There are no exercises that can be given to students to practice the skill of analysis because there are no such generic skills. Skills are particular facilities, not general abilities (Daniels, 1975). Norris and Ennis (1989) pointed out that not only are Bloom's (1956) categories problematic because of their vagueness and overlap, they also were never intended to serve as a source for lists of critical thinking skills.

According to Court (1991), views on critical thinking have matured, and today few people are enamored of this isolated approach. Nevertheless, lists of skills still appear in virtually every curriculum guide. There may be aspects of thinking that can be called skills, but we need to continue to move away from the idea that good thinking involves a set of skills. Based on Court, a recent social studies curriculum guide lists under citizenship skills the skill of self-worth, a ludicrous misuse of the word skill (pp. 115-119).

Problem Solving Approach

According to Selman (1989), another approach to teaching critical thinking has been to get students to "engage in systematic, logical thinking to solve problems by following a series of steps" (p. 115). These steps include defining the question or problem and generating hypotheses. These steps are followed by collecting and testing evidence, then by accepting or rejecting the hypotheses. This process could take the form of solving a hypothetical problem connected with a topic being studied in social studies (Selman, 1989).

For example, students studying pioneer life might be asked if it is better for a new pioneer family to build their home near a town, where they can have the ready assistance of neighbors, or should they build it ten miles from town, where they can get more land for their farm? Students "can make a choice, then gather information from books and films, then evaluate their decision in the light of this evidence and alter it if necessary" (Selman, 1989, p. 115).

There has been much debate over whether students should be given hypothetical problems or whether they should be engaged, in Dewey fashion in solving real-life problems that relate to their own experience. According to this approach, students might engage in problem solving about how to reduce fighting on the school grounds, how to set up a welcoming program for new students, or how to reduce paper waste in the classroom (Tanner, 1988).

Although it is unlikely that all critical thinking does or should follow the problem-solving model, it is clearly a useful approach. When "students learn to make judgments and decisions based on good evidence, it seems likely that this process will have application outside of school and later in their lives" (Selman, 1989, p. 116).

According to Selman (1989), the problem solving approach gives them a system by which to identify and solve problems. This approach should also include looking at what counts as good evidence, and articulating the value, both "personal and societal, that underlie judgments that we make" (p. 116). Selman makes the important point that the notion of value free reasoning is a myth and that rather than pretending that our reasoning is based on pure logic alone, we would do well to reflect on and articulate values. If we decide that reducing paper waste in the classroom is a good thing to do, we are operating from a particular value stance. When we are clear about what values are guiding us, we can examine the grounds on which they are held. If under scrutiny they still appear to be valid, we can call on them as part of our reasoning and argument.

Logic Approach

The logic approach equates good thinking with logical thinking. Selman (1989) says of this approach that students are typically taught to identify such logical categories as premises and conclusions, and to convert arguments into deductive form. One might, for instance, bring a problem into relief by stating it in the form of a deductive syllogism.

Information Processing Approach

The information processing approach is part of a broad cognitive science view of thinking that considers understanding and the teaching of good thinking to be the analysis of tasks into components bits of information and processing steps (Selman, 1989). In this vein, William (1989), characterized thinking as people's attempt to search out, describe and explain patterns in the world. In a book for teachers based on this approach, one finds that information processing theory is grounded in the premise that people innately strive to make sense of the world around them.

In an effort to achieve the order they instinctively need, people investigate and structure the experiences they have (Eggan & Kauchak, 1988). Investigation in this way will "observe, compare, find similarities and differences, and form concepts and generalizations based on the similarities" (p. 3), which appears to be an accurate and useful way of looking at how people learn and make meaning of new information. The idea of getting students to "observe, compare, look for relationships is certainly a useful one for helping them learn content" (p. 3). For example, student might be asked to observe and compare, through reading and discussion, the different kinds of food and shelter used by Native Americans in different parts of North America and the ways in which food and shelter are connected with art, religion, and mythology. They might then be guided to the generalization that climate affects culture" (Selman, 1989, p. 117).

In terms of making judgments and decisions, information processing is an incomplete model. Once the appropriate information has been processed and understood through observation and comparison, judgments and decision can be made. Solving the equation of the extent to which old growths forests should be logged or deciding whether the city of Jerusalem should be politically divided, for instance, will never be done on the basis of information and logic alone. Conflicting sets of values are at work in these situations, and those who formulate a solution do so from their particular value position. Achieving workable compromises and finding solutions to pressing real world problems requires more than the ability to observe compare and see patterns. Compromises and solutions involve decision-making and require "originality, diplomacy, tact, and respect for awareness of people's deeply held values, which does not mean that respect for different set of values is the same as complete value relativism" (Selman, 1989, p. 117).

Multi-aspect Approach

What Selman (1989) has termed the multi-aspect approach is based on the identification of the numerous abilities, attitudes, and propensities one must have to be called a good critical thinker. Norris and Ennis (1989), proponents of this approach, defined critical thinking as "reasonable and effective thinking that is focused upon deciding what to believe or do" (p.

3). This list offers analysis of the kind of things an effective thinker can implement. There are some difficulties, however.

What do teachers need to do to foster the development of critical thinkers? It is suggested that teachers should draw from the approaches already in use, however these approaches need to fit into larger visions of what critical thinking classrooms (and, by implication, a critical thinking school and critical thinking society) would look like. Just as vision of an educated person drives our work in curriculum and educational planning, so this vision should drive our attempts to teach critical thinking skills (Norris & Ennis, 1989).

Norris and Ennis' (1989) definition of critical thinking is reasonably and effectively going about deciding what to believe or do that seems like a good beginning. In a critical thinking classroom, there would be ongoing discussions, and compromises. The problems and questions under discussion would be both real world problems about the running of the school and issues in the community and about academic issues related to history, science, mathematics, and art.

A great deal of analysis, discussion, and decision-making is going on in many classrooms. We need to build on this base and allow students more freedom to ask questions, real questions, some of which may threaten the outdated education model in which the ultimate answer is because I said so. None of this means that teachers must relinquish all their authority. It is teachers' responsibility to give "guidance, and sometimes firm guidance, to developing young minds" (Court, 1991, p. 117).

Nonetheless, all topics should be open for discussion, including schools and classrooms rules. Educators should be able to offer students choices and good reasons for rules. The school system is still, to a great extent, authoritarian, right answer slanted, and examination driven; conditions that are not conducive to critical thinking (Court, 1991). These structural lags in the system impede teachers who are actively pursuing the goal of achieving a critical thinking oriented classroom.

Good thinking in the classroom is closely connected to how well the people in the classroom are relating to one another. Teachers who respect students and view them as intelligent beings, and worth listening to, will encourage students to ask and investigate. To do this, teachers must be free of shallow accountability, having patience, energy, and high self-esteem. It takes a healthy psyche to relinquish the role of the basis of all knowledge and holder of all authority (Court, 1991).

We must make structural changes that allow teachers time to engage in collegial discussion and reflection; we must have reasonable class size, and we must offer "continued, high quality professional development activities that are concerned with ways of engaging with students on a thinking level" (Court, 1991, p. 118).

The National Center on Education and the Economy (NCEE) (2004), a non-profit organization based in Washington, D. C., believes it is possible for almost everyone to learn far more and develop far higher skills than most of us have thought possible. The hallmark of the National Center's work is standards-base reform. They believe that education and training systems work best when clear standards, that match the highest in the world are set for student achievement, accurate measures of progress against those standards are devised, the people closest to the students are given the authority for figuring out how to get the students to the standards and are then held accountable for students progress (p. 1).

The NCEE also believes that learning systems cannot be effective unless the students themselves ultimately assume responsibility for their own learning and the system is designed so that they will do so. NCEE also believes that students of all ages learn best when they can see the purpose of their learning and are constantly putting what they are learning to work.

Most of all, NCEE believes that if they expect more of people, they expect more of themselves.

Definition of Critical Thinking

There are many definitions of critical thinking. Paul (1988) states that critical thinking is "the ability of students to reach sound conclusions based on observations and information" (p. 49). Ennis (1987) suggests that critical thinking is reasonable, reflective thinking that is focused on deciding what to believe or do (pp. 49-51).

Font, Todd, and Welch (1996) define critical thinking as the ability to think about one's own thinking process. Paul (1988) defines critical thinking as the intellectually discipline process of actively conceptualizing, applying, analyzing, synthesizing, and/or evaluating information gathered by observation, experience, reflection, reasoning, or communication, as a guide to brief and action (pp. 49-51).

Beyer (1983) describes it as assessing the "authenticity, accuracy, and worth of knowledge, claims, beliefs, or arguments" (pp. 41, 44-49). Norris (1985) states that "critical thinking helps students to apply everything students already know and feel, to evaluate their own thinking, and especially to change their behavior" (pp. 40-45).

Critical thinking is synonymous with the terms analytical reasoning, synthesis, problem-solving, or higher mental processes (Scriven & Paul, 1992). Critical thinking was assumed to develop automatically with acquired knowledge. Yet, in order to improve students' critical thinking skills, critical thinking must be measured and defined before developing and testing empirical intervention strategies to promote students' critical thinking skills in all grade levels (Hummel & Huitt, 1994).

Paul (2005) defines critical thinking as (a) disciplined, self-directed thinking that exemplifies the perfections of thinking appropriate to a particular mode or domain of thinking, (b) thinking that displays mastery of intellectual skills and abilities, and (c) the art of thinking about your thinking (metacognition) while you are thinking in order to make your thinking better, more clear, more accurate, or more defensible (p. 2).

A critical thinker is someone who is able to think well and fair-mindedly, not just about his or her beliefs and viewpoints, but about beliefs and viewpoints that are opposed to his or her own beliefs. A critical thinker is a person who thinks critically is not just willing and able to explore any threatening viewpoints, but he or she desires to do so. A critical thinker suspends judgment (Paul, 2005).

The purpose of teaching critical thinking is to prepare students for a future of effective problem-solving, thoughtful decision-making and lifelong learning. Simply having a skill, such as critical thinking, is no guarantee that a student will use it. In order for skills to become a part of students' daily behavior, students must be cultivated in an environment that values and sustains them (Paul, 2005).

Paul points out that critical thinking strategies enhance content learning. Decision-making strategies can deepen students' thinking about historical and literary decision points covered in the curriculum. Strategies can be constructed to help students study, to help them understand difficult concepts and to tackle other content-related challenges.

Educators can immediately begin improving students' critical thinking skills by implementing basic strategies. First, teachers must ensure that there are instructional objectives for the lesson's content (Wiggins, 1991). Objectives can neither be too broad nor too specific, but specific enough to determine what students should be able to do after mastery of objectives. Next, teachers should evaluate the objectives to determine whether students have mastered the content at the stated level of proficiency. If test items are used that only require lower-level thinking skills on the knowledge and comprehension level, students will not develop and use higher-level thinking skills at the analytical and evaluative level (Hummel & Huitt, 1994).

The Georgia Grade Five Writing Assessment

The Georgia Grade Five Writing Assessment is a test of narrative writing in which the writer tells a real or imagined story. The Georgia Grade Five Writing Assessment assesses two types of narrative writing: telling a personal experience and creating an imaginative story (Georgia Department of Education, 2001).

The State Writing Assessment Advisory Council assisted the Georgia Department of Education in developing the writing component of the student assessment program. The Council, consisting of educators with expertise in the instruction of writing skills or writing assessment, is comprised of a Grade 3 Committee, Grade 5 Committee,

Grade 8 Committee, and Grade 11 Committee
(Georgia Department of Education, 2001).

Section 20-2-281 of the Official Code of Georgia Annotated (O.C.G.A.) requires that writing assessments be administered to students in grades 3, 5, 8, and 11. In the Grade 3 Writing Assessment and Grade 5 Writing Assessment, student writings are evaluated on a developmental stage scoring scale to provide diagnostic feedback to students, parents, and teachers concerning individual student performance. The Middle Grades Writing Assessment (MGWA) provides predictive information on 8th graders about their future writing performance in advance of taking the Georgia High School Writing Test (GHSWT). The GHSWT is administered to 11th grade students to determine their graduation status

Assessment procedures may result in the improvement of writing and writing instruction. Assessment generally reflects a natural integration of the language arts. Assessment conditions should parallel, as closely as possible, the teaching of writing. Assessment may also reflect a writing

process and occur over a period of time, not in a single designated time period (Georgia Department of Education, 2001).

Philosophy of the Georgia Grade Five Writing Assessment

Writing is a process that involves students' discovery of knowledge based on their reading experiences. Students should be encouraged to read and write across the content areas because reading and writing provide students with a sense of growth as it widens students' perspectives on life. Content area writing helps to strengthen students' abilities to synthesize information in a logical and structured manner. Writing in the classroom can reflect what is occurring in the curriculum. As a result, quality writing experiences can ultimately lead to writing success in all content areas (Georgia Department of Education, 2001).

Writing is generally viewed as a developmental process that emerges as children experience language in a real, meaningful, and natural way. Most writing experiences are developmentally appropriate and authentic. Reading, writing, listening, thinking, and speaking are interactive and inseparable and should be taught accordingly. Students learn to write by writing. Writing is an ongoing process. Students may participate in many activities related to the writing process such as talking, reading, planning, brainstorming, collaborating, drafting, revising, sharing, proofreading, publishing, responding, revisiting, and conferencing (Georgia Department of Education, 2001).

The Six Stages of Writing

There are six stages of writing that are used as developmental stage scoring for raters to evaluate students' writing: emerging writer, developing writer, focusing writer, experimenting writer, engaging writer, and the extended writer. All assessment raters must complete a ten-hour training program and pass a qualifying test before scoring actual student papers.

No identifying student information is divulged about the student (Georgia Department of Education, 2001).

Stage 1: Emerging Writer

Students in the emerging stage demonstrate little or no evidence of topic development, organization, and detail. There is little awareness of the audience or the writing task as well as errors that prevent the reader from understanding the writer's message (Georgia Department of Education, 2001).

Stage 2: Developing Writer

The developing writer produces a topic that is beginning to be developed in an organized manner. The student has limited awareness of the audience and/or the writing task and uses simple words and simple sentence patterns. The developing writer's writing sample has errors that interfere with communication (Georgia Department of Education, 2001).

Stage 3: Focusing Writer

The focusing writer demonstrates a clear topic although development of the topic is incomplete. There is evidence of an apparent plan with loosely organized ideas with a sense of audience and the writing task. There are minimal varieties of vocabulary and of sentence patterns with errors that interrupt the flow of communication (Georgia Department of Education, 2001).

Stage 4: Experimenting Writer

Students in the experimenting stage have a clear and developed topic although there is an imbalance in the development of the topic. There is evidence of a clear plan for writing with a beginning, middle, and end although the beginning and/or ending may be awkward. Students in stage 4 are able to write with the audience in mind and experiment with language and sentence patterns. Students' word combinations and word choice may be novel with errors that may interrupt the flow of communication (Georgia Department of Education, 2001).

Stage 5: Engaging Writer

Writing samples produced by students in stage 5 exhibit a topic that is well developed and a writing plan with a clear beginning, middle, and end. Students' ability to organize the topic helps to sustain the writer's purpose. Students use audience awareness techniques that engage the reader. There is evidence of the effective use of varied language and sentence patterns with errors that do not interfere with the reader's understanding of the writer's message (Georgia Department of Education, 2001).

Stage 6: Extending Writer

Students in stage 6 demonstrate a topic that is fully elaborated with rich details. Students' writing samples contain organization that sustains the writer's purpose and moves the reader through the writing sample. There is a sense of audience awareness techniques that engage and sustain the reader's interest in the writing sample. Students use creative and novel language with errors that do not interrupt or interfere with the reader's understanding of the writer's message (Georgia Department of Education, 2001).

As shown in Table 1, the results demonstrated that over a four-year period fifth grade students in the selected school decreased the percentage of students in the lower writing stages 1, 2, and 3 and increased the percentage of students in the higher writing stages 4, 5, and 6. The majority of fifth grade students scored in stages 4 and 5 with a slight decrease from 14.3% in 2003-2004 to 10.1% in 2004-2005. No students scored in the lowest stage as emerging writers.

Table 1. Elementary School Profile of Student Achievement

Grade 5 Writing Assessment:
Percent of 5th Graders in Each Category

Categories of Scaled Scores	2004-2005	2003-2004	2002-2003	2001-2002
Stage 1: The Emerging Writer	0%	0%	0%	0%
Stage 2: The Developing Writer	.7%	.6%	0%	.6%
Stage 3: The Focusing Writer	8.6%	10.6%	14.8%	23%
Stage 4: The Experimenting Writer	41.0%	33.5%	43.8%	23%
Stage 5: The Engaging Writer	39.6%	41.0%	34.1%	21.8%
Stage 6: The Extending Writer	10.1%	14.3%	7.4%	7.9%

Beginning to Write

The Georgia Grade Five Writing Assessment is part of Georgia's assessment program, mandated by state law, which also requires testing in the third, fifth, eighth, and eleventh grades. The Georgia High School Writing Test is administered in the eleventh grade and is a graduation requirement (Georgia Department of Education, 2001).

Session One

There are two sessions during the test. Session One is the planning/pre-writing portion that requires students to read the entire topic carefully, then read it again, and think about some possible ideas and details about the topic. The student plans the story before writing the first draft for ten minutes. During the drafting portion, students organize ideas from pre-writing and begin writing the first draft of the story, re-read the topic to be sure the story is about the assigned topic. After 35 minutes, the student finishes the first draft (Georgia Department of Education, 2001).

Session Two

During Session Two of revising and editing, students re-read the topic, read and revise the story, and are certain to include sufficient details to make the story complete. The student is encouraged to use interesting words such as adjectives to describe their writing during the 20 minutes to revise and edit the writing sample. The student then has 20 minutes to complete the final draft by copying the story into the response booklet. Students are given another 5 minutes to proofread the writing sample for mistakes and neatly make any corrections (Georgia Department of Education, 2001).

Students must learn to read and interpret the topic independently. During the assessment, the teacher cannot assist or coach with student interpretations of the writing topic. The teacher may use the sample topics in the guide to make certain the students understand the format and purpose of the writing topic as well as encourage students to read the entire topic before they begin pre-writing (Georgia Department of Education, 2001).

The teacher models the think-aloud about a writing topic and how the topic can become a story. The teacher facilitates a student think-aloud about understanding of a writing topic. Students are encouraged to use visual imagery to develop initial graphic organizers based on their own interpretation of a writing topic. Students share their independent writing samples. Teachers also help students become aware that an audience must be considered when developing their story. In order to sharpen students' awareness of audience, the teacher has students to experiment with writing for different audiences using the same topic. Different groups can write to different audiences and then share with the entire class to discover how an audience reacts to the story (Georgia Department of Education, 2001).

Steps of the Writing Process

Graves (1983) defines the writing process as stages of pre-writing, drafting, revising, editing, and publishing. During the pre-writing stage, the student prepares to write, which is the time that the student selects a topic on what they will write about, reasons why they are writing such as to entertain, inform, persuade, the type of writing such as poetry, narrative, and expository, the audience such as peer groups, adults, and children. Then the student drafts a writing sample, revises and edits, and then publishes the final draft.

Writing is a process. Until the late 1960s and the early 1970s, teachers and students were commonly taught about the tools of the craft of writing such as grammar, punctuation, spelling, usage, and handwriting. Writers use a process that typically includes pre-writing, drafting, revising and editing, writing final draft, and proofreading (Georgia Department of Education, 2001; Volcano, 2005).

Pre-writing Step

Pre-writing is the first important step in producing a well-written story. Teachers lead students through the pre-writing process to help students to carefully read the writing topic and brainstorm several possible ideas. After keeping the topic in mind, the student will select the topic idea that best suits the audience and purpose of the story (Georgia Department of Education, 2001). Before students begin writing, they should think about what they want to write. Students can make a story web or compose a list of their ideas and organize these ideas graphically (ThinkQuest, 2005).

Using imagination, students may compose a list of relevant ideas and details that relate to the assigned writing topic and the preferred story idea.

Students then consider the audience, purpose of writing, characters in their story, setting of story, description of characters, problem or situation, adding events to make the story interesting, and the story conclusion (Georgia Department of Education, 2001).

Students use graphic or visual organizers to arrange the details in their story. Examples of graphic organizers are story chart, clustering, webbing, mapping, and branching (Georgia Department of Education, 2001). During pre-writing, as students prepare to write, they are able to read, think, and free-write in a journal format, identify the purpose of writing and the audience, research, take notes, and gather information. Students are also able to brainstorm with a peer group and organize their thinking as they develop a plan for what they will write about (Volcano, 2005).

According to Graves (1983), pre-writing is a tool that students use to begin to organize their ideas on a topic before they begin to write. Students may select their own topics or teachers may give students specific topics or prompts to write about. Students may organize their thoughts during the pre-writing stage by drawing, talking, brainstorming, reading, semantic mapping, quick writing, and outlining.

The Writing Notebook is a collection of students' ideas, impressions, and writing. While the Writing Notebook is not a journal for recording unrelated ideas, the notebook contains ideas that can be formed into a published piece of writing at a later date (Graves, 1983). Real authors use the Writing Notebook as a place to begin to write about their lives. Students may carry these notebooks with them at all times as they begin to collect pieces of their lives (Graves, 1983).

According to Short, Harste, and Burke (1996), real writers spend a lot of their time collecting pieces of their lives based on personal "observations, memories, ideas, favorite quotes, and clippings from articles from magazines and newspapers" (p. 93). Real writers record observations of people, places, or things in their lives, conversations heard and conversations that they have had with other people. Students may use the Writing Notebook as a sketch pad to draw and illustrate their life experiences. Calkins and Harwayne (1991) reported that the notebook is an invitation to write without any external motivation and the notes taken in the notebook serve as "seeds for publishing writing" (p. 51).

Drafting Step

Drafting consists of putting thoughts on paper. Students focus on the quality and quantity of content as they compose freely without concern for mechanics of grammar (Volcano, 2005). The drafting step involves writing the first draft. Students then put all of their ideas into paragraph form (ThinkQuest, 2005).

During the drafting step, students begin the process of actually writing. Refining their writing sample may require several drafts. The basic premise is for students to get their ideas down on paper rather than be overly concerned at this point with correct spelling, grammar, and punctuation (University of Wisconsin, 2005).

Revising and Editing Step

Revising and editing are critical steps in the writing process in which the student improves the paper. During this step, the student makes sure that all the important points about the subject are made and that the reader can understand all of the ideas. Students finally consider sentence variation, details, transitions, precise language, varied word choice, openings, and endings in their writing samples (Georgia Department of Education, 2001).

Effective ways to begin a story are to write a quote or surprising fact, present an interesting question, write a dialogue between two people, and present a dramatic moment. Effective ways to end a story are to repeat the main idea in a new way, express personal thoughts and feelings about the topic, and tell the last event of the story (Georgia Department of Education, 2001).

During the revising and editing step, students should consider if the story was introduced in an interesting way, details supported the topic sentences, details were easy to follow by the audience, added sensory words or details, summary included personal thoughts and feelings, and the writing sample was checked for errors in capitalization, spelling, punctuation, and grammar and usage (Georgia Department of Education, 2001).

During the revising and editing stage, students take another look at their writing sample while maintaining focus on the content as they share with their peer group or the teacher. Then the student may add, delete, rearrange, and revise the first draft of the writing sample (Volcano, 2005). After students have written the rough draft and edit their story, students may get someone else to read the entire story to check for spelling, punctuation, grammar, and usage (ThinkQuest, 2005).

Students may place emphasis on refining their writing sample as they re-read, share their draft with others, reorganize paragraphs, and make necessary revisions. When revising, students put their writing sample aside for a while and then return to their draft. Students may elect to share their drafts with their peers or the teacher and the ultimate decision to make suggested revisions is left with the student who takes ownership of the writing sample (University of Wisconsin, 2005).

During the editing process, students prepare their writing sample into a final paper. Students may focus on spelling, grammar, usage, punctuation, and mechanics at this stage of the writing process and on the writing sample as being readable for the intended audience (University of Wisconsin, 2005).

Writing Final Draft and Proofreading

Students will write their final draft after proofreading their writing sample. Proofreading is the last step of the writing process. In other words, proofreading is the final polishing and cleaning up of the student's piece of writing before its presentation. Before proofreading, the student completes the earlier stages of pre-writing, drafting, revising, and editing. During proofreading, the student does a final check for errors in omitted or repeated words, capitalization, spelling, grammar and usage, and punctuation (Georgia Department of Education, 2001).

Proofreading occurs during the final draft. Proofreading is a unique type of reading in which the reader reads slowly and concentrates on the mechanics of writing such as the spelling, grammar, and the mechanics of writing. Publishing is considered the final stage of the writing process, which is a time that students prepare their writing sample for an intended audience (University of Wisconsin, 2005).

Writing Workshop

Writing Workshop is an instructional arrangement that is used for students to learn about the writing process and includes time for students to write (Calkins, 1986). Writing Workshop is a term that was coined by Calkins (1986), which means a time set aside for students to participate in and study the writing process. The first and foremost element of Writing Workshop is a predictable time and schedule for writing or a special time of the day that has been set aside especially for writing as students expect and anticipate this time for writing. There are three phases to Writing Workshop: (1) mini-lesson, (2) Writing Workshop, and (3) sharing time.

Mini-lesson

The mini-lesson is guided and directed by the teacher who discusses the conventions of writing. The mini-lesson is a demonstration on how writers write that can be introduced at the beginning, middle, or end of the mini-lesson. The topic of the mini-lesson is based on the teacher's observations of what students are doing with the writing process and their level of development in the writing process (University of Wisconsin, 2005).

Mini-lessons are brief and focus on format, and expand and extend the student's writing. Mini-lessons also consist of writing time and conferencing when students write on selected topics. During Writing Workshop, the writing process steps are emphasized with pre-writing, drafting, revising, editing, and publishing.

Conferencing occurs to show students what they know about writing and what they are writing about (Graves, 1994). During conferencing, a student leader is selected either by the group or the teacher to lead the discussions, sharing time, and determine the focus in the group. There are two types of conferences: nudging and process. Nudging conferences may be needed to help students to browse through their Writing Notebooks to come up with a writing topic. Process conferences can take place at any time during the process of writing during pre-writing, drafting, revising, editing, and publishing (University of Wisconsin, 2005).

Mini-lessons can include information regarding the schedule, days and time of the workshop, writing notebooks, modeling writing techniques such as openings, sketching characters, using imagery, incorporating figurative language, or conventions of writing in writing a letter or a poem (Pappas, Kiefer, & Levstid, 1995). Mini-lessons include five steps: (1) introducing the strategy, (2) demonstrating the strategy, (3) practicing the strategy, (4) reviewing the strategy, and (5) practicing the strategy (University of Wisconsin, 2005).

Introducing the Strategy

During this strategy, the teacher introduces to students what they will be learning and why they will be learning this strategy (University of Wisconsin, 2005).

Demonstrating the Strategy

The teacher models or demonstrates how students should use this strategy. The teacher may develop a piece of writing to share with the students. The teacher may also use an artifact such as a letter, a book, or a report written by another writer. Then the teacher demonstrates how authors of published works have used this strategy (University of Wisconsin, 2005).

Practicing the Strategy

During this phase, students are given the opportunity to practice this strategy in their writing. The teacher may provide a writing prompt for students or students may select a topic of their choice. Students should use each step of the writing process as they write.

The Process Writing Classroom

Teachers in a process writing classroom observe students' writing behaviors and facilitate instructional strategies that will help the students become better writers by recognizing their strengths, modeling appropriate strategies, and evaluating what the student is actually doing in writing. Based on these observations, teachers plan instruction that extends and expands students' written language. Observation and evaluation should occur in four areas: (1) development of text and text structure, (2) spelling, (3) mechanics, and (4) grammar.

Text Structure

The first part of observation and evaluation involves development of text and text structure, which consist of narrative text and expository text.

Narrative Text

The purpose of narrative text is to entertain, to tell a story, or to provide an aesthetic literary experience. Narrative text is based on students' life experiences and is person-oriented using dialogue and familiar language (Tonjes, Wolpow, & Zintz, 1999). Examples of narrative test are folk tales such as legends, myths, tall tales, fables, contemporary fiction, mysteries, science fiction, realistic fiction, fantasy, and historical fiction (University of Wisconsin, 2005).

Story grammar is the knowledge of how stories are organized with the beginning of the story consisting of the setting, the characters, and problems of characters. The middle of the narrative is centered on the plot, which includes a series of episodes that are written by the student to hold the audience's attention and build excitement as the story unfolds. The ending of the story contains the resolution or solution to the problem of the character and the conclusion to the story (University of Wisconsin, 2005).

Expository Text

Expository text is written by authors to inform, explain, describe, present information or to persuade. Expository text is subject-oriented and contains facts and information using little dialogue (Tonjes, Wolpow, & Zintz, 1999). The organization of the structure of expository text depends on the genre such as letter, journal entry, newspaper article, editorial, brochure, map, etc. Heller (1995) reported that there were seven types of text structures: definition, description, process or time order, classification, comparison, analysis, and persuasion.

Definition is the form of writing that authors use when they want to define a topic or subject. Definitions are especially important part of any type of writing such as expository text (Heller, 1995). Description is a form of writing that is used to describe the attributes and features of people, places or items. Usually in descriptive writing, the main topic is introduced and then the attributes are included in the body of the paragraph. A graphic organizer may be used to outline the individual characteristics of the topic being introduced. Process or time order is a form of writing that is used if the author wishes to inform readers about specific topics by listing events or steps in chronological order. Words that signal this type of text structure are first, next, before, and after (University of Wisconsin, 2005).

Classification allows students to classify events by likes and dislikes to help with the understanding of text structure (Heller, 1995). Comparison text demonstrates to students how two or more people, places, or things are similar and different. Authors use descriptions of the items being compared to illustrate the differences or similarities of items being compared (University of Wisconsin, 2005).

Analysis text is used to discuss cause and effect or problems and the solutions. Authors use problem-solution when they present a problem and include the possible solutions to this problem. Heller (1995) states that "when analyzing a topic, the author or reader examines the relationships between the parts and the whole in order to communicate or comprehend the structure of the underlying ideas" (p. 152). Persuasive writing is used to convince the reader to view things from the author's point of view. Persuasive writing is used by authors to present arguments or to express their point of view (University of Wisconsin, 2005).

Spelling

The second part of observation and evaluation involves spelling errors while writing, which consist of analysis of spelling errors and development of spelling.

Analysis of Spelling Errors

When analyzing the development of spelling, the analysis includes two dimensions such as identifying the stage of spelling development and analyzing the spelling errors. The spelling errors are classified as pre-phonetic spelling, phonetic spelling, or transitional spelling. To calculate the student's spelling level, figure the total number of words in the selection being analyzed. Next, determine the total percent of correct words in the selection. Finally, chart the spelling errors in the categories pre-phonetic, phonetic, or transitional (University of Wisconsin, 2005).

Development of Spelling

Gentry and Gillet (1993) identified five stages of spelling development: pre-communicative, semi-phonetic, phonetic, transitional, and correct. Pre-communicative stage means spelling that cannot be read by others and is often called the babbling stage of spelling. Students in this stage attempt to communicate a message but the student is the only one who can read and understand the message. Instruction at this stage should focus on the teacher modeling reading and writing by reading aloud, language experience stories that are dictated by the read to the teacher, daily writing, labeling the environment, and shared book experiences (University of Wisconsin, 2005).

In the semi-phonetic or pre-phonetic stage, students know that there are letters in words but they spell words in an abbreviated way by illustrating a beginning understanding of the sounds associated with the written letters. However, others will have difficulty reading the student's words at this stage. Instruction at this stage should provide experiences that involve reading and writing and the teacher modeling the reading and writing. Students in this stage will benefit from word walls, patterned language, language experience, and reading aloud and writing (University of Wisconsin, 2005).

In the phonetic stage, the student's spelling does not conform to standard English spellings, but the spelling is similar to the correct spelling and can be read and deciphered by the reader. In this stage, students spell words the way they sound. Instruction should focus on exploring sound relationships with long and short vowel sounds, beginning sounds, rhyming words, phonemic awareness activities, onset-rime, and playing with language (University of Wisconsin, 2005).

In the transitional stage, the student is beginning to spell more words correctly and incorrectly. The student realizes that words must be spelled not only on the basis of how they sound, but also based on how they look. During this stage, words spelled by students look as close to the real word as possible. Instruction in the transitional stage should emphasize short and long vowels, rubber banding words, consonant blends, spelling strategies, proofreading, plurals of irregular words, words that end with 'er' or 'or', and compound words (University of Wisconsin, 2005).

Conventional or correct spelling stage is where the student is correctly spelling 90 percent of the words in the writing sample. Formal instruction in spelling begins in the conventional stage. Students understand the English system and how it works. Instruction at this level should focus on the structure of prefixes and suffixes, doubling consonants rules for words ending in *ing, ed, er, est,* common irregular spellings, possessives, using base words to form new words, dictionary skills, proofreading, editing, rubber banding words, and the spelling error patterns (University of Wisconsin, 2005).

Mechanics of Writing

The third part of observation and evaluation involves the mechanics of writing, which is used to analyze the student's understanding of the mechanics of writing. The mechanics of writing includes punctuation such as use of periods, question marks, exclamation marks, commas, apostrophes, quotation marks, and capital letters (University of Wisconsin, 2005).

Grammar of the English Language

The fourth part of observation and evaluation involves the analysis of the student's use of the grammar of the English language. To evaluate the grammatical structures in students' written language, students should construct connected discourse in two levels. The primary level is for students in first through third grades and intermediate level is for students in fourth through sixth grade (University of Wisconsin, 2005).

America's Choice Program

The National Center on Education and the Economy (NCEE) (2004) established the America's Choice School Design in 1989. Presently, there are 650 schools, including charter schools in 16 states that are implementing America's Choice School Design. The primary goal is to enable all students to reach internationally benchmarked standards in English, mathematics, and science. The main features of the program are performance standards and reference examinations. Five key design tasks are standards and assessments, student learning, teacher training, community supports, and parent-public involvement (Appalachia Educational Laboratory-AEL, 2005a).

America's Choice, a standards-based reform program is being implemented in Laurens County because the program's reading and writing curriculum would help the district to accomplish the goal of having students to compete with their peers throughout the world. The comprehensive school design exemplifies what students should know and be able to do at the third, fifth, eighth, and eleventh grades.

The No Child Left Behind Act (NCLB) of 2001 is placing new requirements on teachers and new standards on students. The America's Choice school design assists states, districts and schools to meet these requirements. America's Choice is built on the premise that teaching to explicit standards is the best strategy for disadvantaged and low-performing students. The America's Choice staff works with schools to link its performance to state content standards (Appalachia Educational Laboratory-AEL, 2005a).

The America's Choice School Design incorporates a standards-based curriculum that focuses on the basics, conceptual mastery, and applications that include a design for quickly identifying students who are falling behind and bringing them back to standard. The program also includes a planning and management system for making the most efficient use of available resources to raise student performance quickly. The program focuses in the early years on literacy in reading, writing, and mathematics (AEL, 2005a).

Research Related to America's Choice School Design

Results in schools in Kentucky and Chicago reveal significant improvement in scores on standardized tests. Of the 15 schools in Kentucky, 87 percent earned cash rewards in 1995, the first year of the state's incentive program, compared with 38 percent of schools statewide. From 1992 to 1996, an average of 74 percent of Kentucky's schools met or exceeded their performance goals (AEL, 2005a, p. 1).

In Chicago, about 80 percent of America's Choice schools showed significant increases in their citywide test scores. In one year, these schools had significant increases in fourth, eighth, and tenth grade performance on the New Standards Reference Examinations in language arts and mathematics (AEL, 2005a, p. 1).

In 1998, six schools in Rochester, New York were among the national's finest schools to adopt the America's Choice school improvement program. NCEE contracted with the Consortium for Policy Research Evaluation (CPRE) to evaluate the America's Choice School Design. The test scores of students of students in America's Choice schools to those in other schools revealed that America's Choice students outperformed their peers by an average of 17 percent a year in reading in grades 4 and 8.

The minority gap between Black and Hispanic students and White decreased in America's Choice schools. The program was significant for the city's lowest performing students. The bottom 25 percent of students in America's Choice schools gained significantly more than did the lowest performing students attending non-America's Choice schools. A study of 232 school reforms conducted by the University of Wisconsin found that on the average an America's Choice student at the 50th percentile would have moved to the 60th percentile on standardized tests in one year (NCEE, 2004, p. 1).

History of Appalachia Educational Laboratory (AEL)

AEL is a non-profit 501(c)3 corporation that provides education research, development, professional development, and consulting services in the pre-kindergarten through grade 12. The name AEL originated with the first program the corporation operated in 1966 as the Appalachia Educational Laboratory, but today AEL is national in scope and provides a range of services to private and government agencies. The corporation is known as AEL and the laboratory program, which continues to be operated by AEL, is referred to as the Regional Educational Laboratory at AEL (AEL, 2005a).

Summary

Critical thinking is the "intellectually disciplined process of actively and skillfully conceptualizing, applying, analyzing, synthesizing, and/ or evaluating information gather from, or generated by, observation, experience, reflection, reasoning, or communication as a guide to belief and action" (Scriven & Paul, 2004, p. 1).

Because everyone thinks due to their nature to think, much of people's thinking involves critical thinking. Critical thinking is a particular mode of thinking about any content, any subject, or any problem in which the thinker "improves the quality of his or her thinking" (Scriven & Paul, 2004, p. 1). Critical thinking involves being able to communicate effectively as one attempts to solve problems (Scriven & Paul).

The No Child Left Behind Act (NCLB) of 2001 challenges schools and school districts to explore strategies that can help all students improve their academic performance in reading, mathematics, language arts, science, and social studies. Through staff development activities in critical thinking, teachers will learn to expand their knowledge of the link between "quality questioning" and achievement by all students (AEL, 2005b, p. 1).

participants were selected because they were trained using the America's Choice program materials and instructional methods.

Two student focus groups included Student Focus Group 1 with three selected students who were participants in the America's Choice program during 2004-2005. Student Focus Group 2 consisted of three selected students who were not participants in the America's Choice program during 2004-2005, but participated in a regular writing program. The researcher selected the students based on the criteria of students' ability to express themselves orally and in writing. In addition, parental consent forms were obtained for each student.

Fifth grade students' composite writing scores from the Georgia Grade Five Writing Assessment scores were examined and analyzed to determine the percentage of students who scored in the highest and lowest stages of writing.

The criteria for the student population for this study consisted of students who attended the selected elementary school during 2004-2005 and took the Grade Five Writing Assessment. The population also included students who were served in the Program for Exceptional Children (PEC), unless otherwise documented in the child's Individualized Education Program (IEP) by the testing date of January 18, 2005. Section 20-2-281 of the O.C.G.A. (Official Code of Georgia Annotated) requires that writing assessments be administered to students in grades three, five, eight, and eleven. The goal of the Writing Assessment was to determine the writing level of students in order to design instruction for improving their writing skills.

The researcher is an employee at this elementary school and the sample population is called a convenience sampling because the selected teachers are also employees at this school and selected students in this study attend this school.

The researcher did not present questions to the focus group. Another teacher with a post-graduate degree from a different school agreed to conduct the teachers' focus group interview in order to avoid any compromise to the integrity of this research or any coercion that may result from participating in the study. The focus group lasted approximately 60 minutes.

Teachers in grade 5 who returned their consent forms, had used materials, supplies, and were trained to use instructional methods from the America's Choice program requirements were administered a teacher survey at the end of a scheduled faculty meeting. The researcher provided the purpose of this research study and outlined procedures for completing the survey. The completion of the survey took approximately 30 minutes. Surveys were individually and sequentially numbered for tracking purposes only. No names were used on the teacher survey. All data will be destroyed three years after the study. All data was kept confidential.

Finally, collection of student writing data included examining and analyzing the composite writing scores of 185 fifth grade students using descriptive statistics based on established criteria from the Georgia Grade Five Writing Assessment during 2004-2005.

Although the interview was audio-taped and teachers' comments were later transcribed, there were no identifying marks to indicate which comments belonged to which teacher and anonymity of teachers was maintained.

Teachers in the focus group interview were given pseudonyms to maintain anonymity. During and after transcription of the audio-tapes, all documents, including audio-tapes and transcripts were secured in a locked safe only accessible to the researcher and destroyed three years after the conclusion of this study.

All participants were asked to maintain full confidentiality concerning their survey responses and oral responses in the focus group. Each teacher participant signed a letter of informed consent.

Three students were selected by the researcher to participate in Student Focus Group 1 that participated in America's Choice program and three students who did not participate in America's Choice program during 2004-2005 comprised Student Focus Group 2. Criteria for selection were students' ability in oral and written expression. Parental permission forms were obtained. Student assent forms were completed and returned by these students. The interview took approximately 60 minutes during school time.

Since the researcher used only the composite scores of 185 fifth grade students and not individual student's scores, parent permission was not required for the analysis of composite test data. Permission from the school principal and school district was needed, requested, and received.

America's Choice Elementary Instructional Program

The centerpiece of the America's Choice elementary instructional program is an extended daily literacy block. Students in grades 4-5 take classes that are two hours long and emphasize reading and writing. The skills development provides systematic instruction in the essential components of literacy. In reading, the workshop classroom format is used. Concentration is on oral language development, vocabulary instruction, comprehension, and the development of fluency in reading. The daily session includes rituals and routines such as reading to children, shared or choral reading and teacher led instruction to small and large groups, as well as partner reading and independent reading with guidance and feedback.

According to the State Writing Assessment Advisory Council and the Georgia Department of Education, writing is a process of discovery which transcends the classroom. They also believe young writers should be encouraged to read across the disciplines because a wide range of reading experiences provides topics and issues for writing, gives students a sense of the nature of written language, and opens up perspectives of the wider world. Next, content are writing strengthen students' abilities to synthesize information in a logical and organized manner; therefore, writing in the classroom can reflect learning that is occurring throughout the curriculum. Finally, frequent, quality writing experiences ultimately lead to writing success.

Instrumentation

The Grade Five Writing Assessment consisted of two 45 minute writing sessions, with the suggestion that students work on two consecutive days so that they had time to think about and revise their initial draft.

Instrumentation 1: Teacher Survey (Quantitative)

A teacher survey (see Appendix A) was developed to describe the critical thinking skills and writing components of America's Choice program. Teachers in grade 5 were asked to complete a survey expressing their opinions about the program's success in influencing fifth grade students' critical thinking and writing skills. Data were analyzed based on a four-point Likert type scale of 4 = Excellent, 3 = Good, 2 = Fair, and 1 = Poor. Data were input into a statistical command package called the Statistical Package of Social Sciences (SPSS) and analyzed using descriptive statistics of frequencies, means, and standard deviations.

Instrumentation 2: Teacher Focus Group (Qualitative)

In addition to the teacher survey, six teachers participated in a focus group (see Appendix B) and expressed their opinions about America's Choice program. The focus group was audio-taped. Questions 1 through 7 were analyzed using 1 = Yes and 0 = No responses. Questions 8 through 15 were analyzed using transcribed data from the tapes and written responses of teachers. Teachers' comments were confidential and there were no identifying marks to determine which comments belonged to particular teachers.

Instrumentation 3: Student Focus Groups (Qualitative)

Two student focus groups (see Appendixes C and D) questions 1 through 9 were analyzed using transcribed data from the tapes and written students' responses. Three students comprised Student Focus Group 1. These students were participants in the America's Choice program during 2004-2005. Three students comprised formed Student Focus Group 2. These students were not participants in the America's Choice program during 2004-2005, but participated in a regular writing program.

Instrumentation 4: Writing Scores of 5th Grade Students (Quantitative)

One hundred and eighty five fifth grade students' composite writing scores were evaluated based on the criteria previously established by the Georgia Grade Five Writing Assessment. Descriptive statistics using percentages were used to describe fifth grade students' writing scores.

CHAPTER FOUR

RESULTS

Introduction

Chapter four discusses the analyses of data of a teacher survey regarding the impact of America's Choice program on fifth grade students' composite writing scores from the Georgia Fifth Grade Writing Assessment, and a teacher focus group of teachers and two focus groups of students. The teacher survey, teacher focus group and two student focus groups provided their written and oral perceptions of the America's Choice program and its benefits to the critical thinking and writing skills of fifth grade students. Three students comprised Student Focus Group 1. These students were participants in the America's Choice program during 2004-2005. Three students comprised formed Student Focus Group 2. These students were not participants in the America's Choice program, but were participants in a regular writing program.

A teacher survey was analyzed regarding America's Choice impact on fifth grade students' critical thinking and writing skills. An analysis of data utilized descriptive statistics of teachers' responses to survey items. In addition to the survey, a teacher focus group met and discussed 15 questions. Their responses were audio-taped to ensure accuracy of teachers' comments. Questions 1 through 7 were required a yes or no response and were analyzed using the ratings of 1 = Yes and 0 = No. Questions 8 through 15 were analyzed using transcribed data from the tapes and written responses of teachers.

Table 6 presents data to support that approximately 83 percent of the teachers believe that fifth grade students have a good ability to transmit information and knowledge effectively. Seventeen percent of the teachers reported that students' ability was fair.

Table 6. Ability to Transmit Information/Knowledge Effectively

Students have the ability to transmit information/knowldege effectively.

					Cumulative
Valid	Fair	1	16.7	16.7	16.7
	Good	5	83.3	83.3	100.0
	Total	6	100.0	100.0	

Approximately sixty-seven percent of the teachers reported that fifth grade students' ability to understand what they read was good, while slightly more than 33 percent felt that students have an excellent ability to understand what they read (see Table 7).

Table 7. Ability to Understand What They Read

Students have the ability to understand what they read.

					Cumulative
Valid	Good	4	66.7	66.7	66.7
	Excellent	2	33.3	33.3	100.0
	Total	6	100.0	100.0	

Approximately 67 percent of the teachers reported that students have a good ability to move from instructions and concepts to execution of projects independently compared to slightly more than 33 percent who believed that students' ability to perform this task was fair (see Table 8).

Table 8. Ability to Move from Instructions and Concepts to Execution of Projects Independently

Students have the ability to move from instructions and concepts to execution of projects independently.

					Cumulative
Valid	Fair	2	33.3	33.3	33.3
	Good	4	66.7	66.7	100.0
	Total	6	100.0	100.0	

Teachers were in complete agreement that fifth grade students have good ability to use general concepts in the content areas. One hundred percent of the teachers reported that students have good ability to use general concepts in the content areas (see Table 9).

Table 9. Ability to Use General Concepts in Content Areas

Students have the ability to use general concepts in content areas.

					Cumulative
Valid	Good	6	100.0	100.0	100.0

One hundred percent of the teachers reported that students have good ability to use appropriate vocabulary during writing in the content areas (see Table 10).

Table 10. Ability to Use Appropriate Vocabulary during Writing in the Content Areas

Students have the ability to use appropriate vocabulary during writing in the content areas.

				Cumulative
Valid Good	6	100.0	100.0	100.0

Eighty-three percent of the teachers felt that fifth grade students had good critical thinking skills while approximately 17 percent believed that students had fair critical thinking skills (see Table 11).

Table 11. Rating of Students' Critical Thinking Skills

Rate your students critical thinking skills.

				Cumulative
Valid Fair	1	16.7	16.7	16.7
Good	5	83.3	83.3	100.0
Total	6	100.0	100.0	

Eighty-three percent of the teachers reported that America's Choice was good as it benefited fifth grade students' writing skills and 17 percent of the teachers believed that America's Choice was fair in providing benefits to fifth grade students' writing skills (see Table 12).

Table 12. America's Choice Program Benefited Writing Skills

The America's Choice Program has benefited my students writing skills

					Cumulative
Valid	Fair	1	16.7	16.7	16.7
	Good	5	83.3	83.3	100.0
	Total	6	100.0	100.0	

Table 13 describes the results of teachers' opinions about America's Choice benefiting fifth grade students' critical thinking skills. Slightly more than 83 percent of the teachers felt that America's Choice was good for fifth grade students' critical thinking skills. Approximately 17 percent reported that the program was fair for fifth grade students' critical thinking skills.

Table 13. America's Choice Program Benefited Critical Thinking Skills

The America's Choice Program has benefited my students critical thinking skills.

					Cumulative
Valid	Fair	1	16.7	16.7	16.7
	Good	5	83.3	83.3	100.0
	Total	6	100.0	100.0	

Approximately 67 percent of the teachers believed that the America's Choice program was good in providing staff development for teachers while slightly more than 33 percent stated that the program was fair (see Table 14).

Table 14. America's Choice Program Provided Staff Development for Teachers

The America's Choice program provided ongoing statt development for teachers

					Cumulative
Valid	Fair	2	33.3	33.3	33.3
	Good	4	66.7	66.7	100.0
	Total	6	100.0	100.0	

Slightly more than 83 percent of the teachers felt that overall, the America's Choice program was good in benefiting fifth graders' critical thinking and writing skills, while 17 percent stated that the program was fair (see Table 15).

Table 15. America's Choice Program Beneficial to Fifth Graders

Overall, the America's Choice Program is beneficial to fifth grades

					Cumulative
Valid	Fair	1	16.7	16.7	16.7
	Good	5	83.3	83.3	100.0
	Total	6	100.0	100.0	

Research Question Two: Were there differences in teachers' opinions regarding 5th grade students' critical thinking skills as a result of their participation in the America's Choice program?

Analysis of Teacher Focus Group: Questions 1 through 7

When asked if teachers initially interested in the America's Choice curriculum, 67 percent stated that they had no initial interest in the program compared with slightly more than one-third who stated that they were initially interested in the program (see Table 16).

Table 16. Interest in America's Choice Curriculum

Were you initially interested in the America's Choice curriculum?

					Cumulative
Valid	No	4	66.7	66.7	66.7
	Yes	2	33.3	33.3	100.0
	Total	6	100.0	100.0	

Eighty-three percent of the teachers went through a training program to teach the America's Choice curriculum while 17 percent did not have the training (see Table 17).

Table 17. America's Choice Curriculum Training Program

Did you go through a training program to teach the America's Choice curriculum?

					Cumulative
Valid	No	1	16.7	16.7	16.7
	Yes	5	83.3	83.3	100.0
	Total	6	100.0	100.0	

One hundred percent of the teachers were trained in the America's Choice program by the Literacy Coach (see Table 18).

Table 18. Training Personnel

If you were trained, who trained you?

				Cumulative
Valid Literacy Coach	6	100.0	100.0	100.0

Sixty-seven percent of the teachers felt that the students whom they taught were experiencing difficulty in writing compared to slightly more than 33 percent believed that the students were not experiencing difficulty in writing (see Table 19).

Table 19. Students Experiencing Difficulty in Writing

Are the students whom you teach experiencing difficulty in writing?

				Cumulative
Valid No	2	33.3	33.3	33.3
Yes	4	66.7	66.7	100.0
Total	6	100.0	100.0	

Approximately 67 percent of the teachers reported that their students were not knowledgeable about how to think critically while slightly more than 33 percent stated that their students were knowledgeable about how to think critically (see Table 20).

Table 20. Students Knowledgeable about Thinking Critically

Were the students whom you teach knowledgeable about how to think critically?

					Cumulative
Valid	No	4	66.7	66.7	66.7
	Yes	2	33.3	33.3	100.0
	Total	6	100.0	100.0	

Before teachers were introduced to the America's Choice program, slightly more than 83 percent reported that they challenged their students to be critical thinkers compared to 17 percent that did not challenge their students to be critical thinkers (see Table 21).

Table 21. Challenge Students to be Critical Thinkers

Before you were introduced to the America's Choice Program, did you challenge your students to be critical thinkers?

					Cumulative
Valid	No	1	16.7	16.7	16.7
	Yes	5	83.3	83.3	100.0
	Total	6	100.0	100.0	

Teachers were equally divided in their opinions about whether or not the America's Choice curriculum had increased their students' critical thinking ability (see Table 22).

Table 22. Increased Students' Critical Thinking Ability

So you feel that the America's Choice curriculum has increased your students critical thinking ability?

					Cumulative
Valid	No	3	50.0	50.0	50.0
	Yes	3	50.0	50.0	100.0
	Total	6	100.0	100.0	

Analysis of Teacher Focus Group: Questions 8 through 15

Question 8: Do you feel that critical thinking and writing are important to elementary school children?

Teacher 1 stated that "critical thinking and writing are vital to elementary school children's overall development." Teacher 2 believed that "students are able to learn sound much quicker when they are able to use them in daily writing." "It will help children to prepare them for later writing and testing" replied Teacher 3. Teacher 4 felt that critical thinking and writing are important because "if elementary means third grade and above, then true writing needs to be implemented in elementary, not primary grades." Teacher 5 responded that critical thinking and writing should occur "only at students' developmental stage." Teacher 6 replied that critical thinking and writing "needs to be on grade level or according to the class type such as Early Intervention Program (EIP). It should be taught at the beginning of grade 3. Lower grades should be able to read first."

Question 9: Indicate three to five things the America's Choice has taught you about teaching writing.

Teacher 1 stated that America's Choice has taught her "to start where the student is and move upward by gradually increasing expectations.

Reading and writing are the two most important skills that teachers can deposit into students' lives. America's Choice also taught me that writing is a craft." "I started teaching writing as a result of 'Wright Group' workshops. I learned to allow students time to write daily using journals and inventive spellings. Students get to practice what they know" stated Teacher 2. The three things that Teacher 3 stated that America's Choice taught her about writing were to encourage the student to write daily, get the students to write their ideas on paper, and if the students can tell their story, then they can write their story." Teacher 4 responded that America's Choice taught her about writing that she should "teach writing step-by-step, be child-centered, and children are allowed to be creative." Teacher 5 stated that America's Choice "did not teach her anything that she did not already know and use in the classroom." Teacher 6 replied that the America's Choice program taught her to "teach writing in steps" and to provide "child-centered activities."

Question 10: Indicate three to five things that the America's Choice program has taught you about teaching critical thinking.

Teacher 1 believed that the "America's Choice program taught me several things about teaching critical thinking. Students can develop confidence in reasoning, develop intellectual courage, think independently, read critically, and generate or assess solutions." Teacher 2 responded that students have to go beyond rote learning to apply what they know in different situations." Teachers should "use questioning to result in open-ended answers." Teacher 3 stated that America's Choice has taught her to "challenge my students to write, proofread, and add more details to their writing, to ask students higher order thinking questions, and to use the Socratic Method in thinking." "Mini-lessons are starters for kids to write. Children are encouraged to write about their experiences. Students have chances to add to or edit their work," added Teacher 4. Teacher

5 replied that the America's Choice program has taught her "nothing" about teaching critical thinking. Teacher 6 felt that critical thinking "activities allow creativity and independent thinking." Critical thinking also "promotes great writing, which allows students to write and expand on their writing."

Question 11: Do you stimulate students' thinking by requiring them to go beyond the factual recall or procedural levels, and engage in higher order thinking, which involves the application, synthesis, and evaluation of knowledge? Please explain.

Teacher 1 explained that she "stimulated students' thinking by providing opportunities for free exploration, asking open-ended questions, and setting the stage for self-monitoring." Teacher 2 responded that "the students write responses to books read. We use graphic organizers and 'Know, Want to Know, Want to Learn' (K-W-L) charts." Teacher 3 stimulates her students to go beyond factual recall by determining what students' responses will be. Teacher 3 stated that "if my students give a yes or no response to a question, I will ask them why did they say 'yes' or why did they say 'no'. I will do this to make them give more details." Teacher 4 stated that "Yes, in everything we do, I try to expand or go beyond students' required level of thinking." Teacher 5 replied that her "students are challenged to do their best." Teacher 6 believed that she tries "to go beyond in every lesson I teach and create real-life experiences to relate to each lesson."

Question 12: How often do you ask your students cognitive memory questions (lower order) and focus on factual recall?

Teacher 1 stated that "I ask my students cognitive memory questions daily to maintain a healthy balance." Teacher 2 replied that she asks "both factual and higher order thinking skills daily." "Daily. However, I will also focus on asking higher order questions for detail or clarity" replied Teacher 3. Teachers 4 and 6 simply stated "Daily in each lesson." Teacher 5 responded that she asks students cognitive memory questions and focus on factual recall "every time the opportunity arises."

Question 13: How much of a challenge is it for you to engage your students in productive questions (For example, attention focus-focusing, measuring, comparison, action, problem posing and reasoning)?

Teacher 1 responded that "the challenge is minimal. Engaging students in productive questioning is a means of assessing students' understanding of specific skills." Teacher 2 replied that "it is not too difficult to ask questions using different formats. Using Bloom's taxonomy helps." Teacher 3 stated that "sometimes it depends on what the lesson or assignment is. If the lesson or topic is familiar to the student, then it is not much of a challenge. But if the students are not familiar with the topic, then it presents a little challenge getting them to visualize." Teacher 4 responded that engaging her students in productive questions is "something I try to do in all subject areas each day." Teacher 5 stated "It is not a challenge. It is every day teaching." "I try to role model self-questioning as I teach. This allows students a great chance to copy and instill this skill within their learning", replied Teacher 6.

Question 14: Did you challenge your students to use different types of thinking to answer questions such as critical thinking, creative thinking, convergent thinking, divergent thinking, inductive thinking, deductive thinking, closed thinking, open questions before the America's Choice? Please explain.

Teacher 1 stated that "I did not challenge my students to answer questions on the various levels prior to the America's Choice because of my limited understanding and my focus on preparing students to pass the

Criterion Referenced Competency Test (CRCT)." Teacher 2 responded that "I learned about Bloom's Taxonomy in college so occasionally I would try to use different questioning techniques." Teacher 3 uses "group discussions and projects as well as oral reports" for her students to use different types of thinking to answer questions. Teacher 4 stated that "Yes, I think to some degree all teachers do this (use different types of thinking to answer questions) even if they are not aware of it." Teacher 5 stated that "Yes, according to their developmental level" questions are asked in different ways. Teacher 6 reported that "Yes, I allowed independent thinking, teacher-oriented questions, open-ended questioning, etc." for her students.

Question 15: How often did you engage students in activities which fostered high-level thinking before the America's Choice program?

Teacher 1 responded that "I now realize that I did not engage my students in activities that fostered high level thinking often enough. I have made adjustments and modifications to my techniques." Teacher 2 stated "I would occasionally use activities to foster higher level thinking." Teacher 3 replied that "I try to infuse this concept daily in my lessons." Teacher 4 stated that "I try to engage students daily to foster a higher level of thinking and even before America's Choice." Teacher 5 stated that she engages students in activities which foster high-level thinking "as often as the opportunity presents itself." Teacher 6 responded that "I tried to engage students each day within each lesson."

Research Question Three: Were there differences in 5th grade students' opinions regarding their writing skills as a result of their participation in the America's Choice program?

Analysis of Student Focus Groups

Two student focus groups (see Appendixes C and D) responded to questions 1 through 9 in separate groups. Data were analyzed using transcripts from the audiotapes and students' written responses. Three students comprised Student Focus Group 1. These students were participants in the America's Choice program. Three students comprised formed Student Focus Group 2. These students were not participants in the America's Choice program.

Student Focus Group 1: America's Choice Program

Question 1: Did you enjoy writing before America's Choice program began? Please explain.

Student 1 responded that "sometimes, it depends on what the topic is" when asked if he/she enjoyed writing before America's Choice program began. Student 2 stated, "No, not really. I only wrote when my teacher asked me to on an assignment." Student 3 replied, "Yes, because I get a chance to share my ideas."

Question 2: Do you feel that working with America's Choice has improved your writing ability? Please explain.

Student 1 said, "I like to use different methods to help my writing be enjoyable." Student 2 stated, "I am able to brainstorm and get my ideas together before I start writing." Student 3 replied, "I am learning how to develop my ideas into a story."

Question 3: Do you feel that you learned anything during the opening meeting? If so, please explain.

Student 1 stated, "The opening meeting is a time when the teacher teaches a new or existing writing assignment or a new one." Student 2 replied, "Yes, this is the time when my teacher teaches a new procedure, craft or skill. The opening meeting of the Writers Workshop last for about 5 to 15 minutes." Student 3 responded, "The opening meeting is a time for my teacher to read a story or poem to the class. I can write an ending or rewrite the entire story. I learned a lot at the opening meeting."

Question 4: What is your task during the work session?

Student 1 stated "During the work session, my task is to improve an existing writing assignment or make up a new one." Student 2 responded that "During the work session I am working on new stories or adding some details to a story that I conference with my teachers about improving what I have already written." Student 3 replied, "I am completing a story I have started or I can write a new story."

Question 5: When you are writing in the work session, does the music by Mozart-"Strengthen the Mind" cause a distraction? Please explain.

Student 1 said, "No, the music is not a distraction. The Mozart is fine but I enjoy the jazz by Nagee or Kenny G. Student 2 responded, "No, because I am used to hearing the music during the work session. I look forward to hearing it. Student 3 replied, "No, I enjoy music. It does not interfere with my writing or thinking."

Question 6: What takes place in the Author's Chair?

Student 1 said, "A classmate is the author and they share their writing with everybody." Student 2 responded that "That is the time when the class shares the stories that they wrote. We listen to what other children have written." Student 3 stated, "In the Author's Chair, we can share a completed story with the class."

Question 7: Do you find the word web to be beneficial before writing?

Student 1 stated, "Webbing helps me to explore a story. We are reading in more detail and assist me in writing my own story." Student 2 said, "Yes, it is like having a variety of topics to choose from. Webbing helps me to get my thoughts together so I can write about the topic." Student 3 replied, "Yes, it helps me to pick and choose ideas or topics from my story."

Question 8: Indicate three to five things that America's Choice taught you about writing?

Student 1 listed the following things: "Good writers write. Do not be ashamed to share my work. Be creative." Student 2 replied, "Writing is a process and takes a lot of steps to do it right. Sometimes you can have more than one draft. You should skip lines when writing so you can make corrections or add information that was left out." Student 3 stated that there are three things: "To brainstorm. Write and worry about spelling later. Always skip lines so I can go back and add more stuff later."

Question 9: Indicate three to five things that America's Choice has taught you about critical thinking.

Student 1 stated that America's Choice had been helpful in "Gather my information and decide if what I have gathered is needed. Ask myself the question, 'what is'. When adding details, ask myself the questions what, when, why, and how." Student 2 replied, "Your first piece of writing will not be your final copy. Improve your writing with details. Using a thesaurus is helpful." Student 3 said, "Good writing can be visualized by seeing what is good about my writing. Be able to think things out. Be prepared to add to my first draft and improve it by making it clear for myself and anybody who wants to read it."

Student Focus Group 2: Non-America's Choice Program

Students in Focus Group 2 did not participate in the America's Choice program. These students were not part of the group of students who participated in the program during 2004-2005.

Question 1: Do you enjoy writing? Explain.

Student 1 stated, "I enjoy writing when I write about my family and friends." Student 2 responded, "I get a chance to write in all my classes like in language arts, reading, social studies, science, and math. I like to write about a lot of different things." Student 3 replied that "Sometimes I like to write about different things and it depends on what I am interested in, then I will write a lot of stuff about the topic."

Question 2: Do you feel that your writing has improved in your 5th grade year? Please explain.

Student 1 felt that "My teachers tell us to write all of the time. They help me to write and they tell me how important it is to learn to write well. They tell me about the writing steps and how to use them." Student 2 explained, "My writing has improved in the different types of sentences. I know how to use the correct punctuation and how to spell words that I did not know." Student 3 said, "My teachers are teaching me how to use correct English and how to write well. I have learned a lot in 5th grade that I didn't know in the other grades."

Question 3: Explain and/or list some of the things you learned in your writing class.

Student 1 explained, "The things that I learned in my writing class have helped me a lot. I know what a personal narrative is. I know how to compare and contrast two different things. My teacher showed us how to use adjectives in our descriptive writing." Student 2 described the

types of writing that were helpful such as "parts of speech, different
of sentences like exclamatory, declaratory, and we learned how to
different kinds of letters like the business letter or the friendly le
wrote a friendly letter to my friend that moved to another school.
my friend." Student 3 replied, "I learned how to use my verbs correct.
how to describe things in my writing by using adjectives. I learned
when to use 'a' and 'an' and how to write better."

Question 4: During your work session, what are you required to do?

Student 1 stated that "the teacher makes us work on a story. Somet
we have to have conferences with the teacher and make changes in
writing." Student 2 said, "I like to finish with my story. Then I can
with the teacher and she helps me to correct my spelling and stuff th
wrong. Then I have to write it over and keep it neat." Student 3 rep.
"Every day I write in my journal and put my thoughts in my journal.
teacher told us not to worry about spelling because we have to get our id
down first. Sometimes, if I want to I can work on a story in my journal
then later type it up on the computer that I will print it out."

Question 5: How do you feel about writing when music is played? Doe
motivate you or distract you? Explain.

Student 1 stated, "I listen to music at home when I do my homewo
It's not Mozart, but rhythm and blues, but listening to Mozart music
quite and soothing and I can really concentrate on my work. It keeps n
from being bored." "Quiet music helps me to think better and I don't wal
my mind to daydream. I enjoy listening to music as I write. Music helps t
calm me down, too" said Student 2. "Sometimes I am motivated by musi
because it helps me to write more and think more. I enjoy the peace and
quiet when the music is playing. Sometimes, it makes me sleepy and I wanl
to lay my head on my desk" replied Student 3.

Question 6: Do you find the word web to be beneficial before writing?

Student 1 responded that "A lot of the time we work on creating the word web together in class. After that, I can begin writing my story because I have a lot of words that I can use in my story." Student 2 stated "The word web is helpful to me when I write my story. It gives me lots of ideas or details when I write because sometimes I can't always think of the words to say and write." Student 3 explained the word web as being beneficial because "It has helped me when I do not have an idea what I am going to write about."

Question 7: Indicate three to five things you learned in your writing class.

Student 1 stated that "I learned to write where my teacher could read my writing because sometimes my writing is messy. Now I write neater and my writing has capital letters and punctuation marks. Sometimes I use the dictionary when I don't know how to spell a word. Sometimes the teacher helps me to spell a word." Student 2 replied that "Before I didn't even know what the parts of speech were. Now I can tell a noun, a verb, and adjective from each other. My teacher tells us how to use adjectives to describe things when I write so others will be able to see what I write in their minds." Student 3 stated, "I hate to write my work over and over again, but I learned how to make corrections in my work or to do it right the first time. But my teacher said that I had to write a final draft using capital letters, and punctuation marks. She made us proofread our work. After awhile, it didn't bother me when I had to write it over because I made it sound better when I did that."

Question 8: Indicate three to five things your teacher has taught you about critical thinking.

Student 1 responded, "My teacher is a good teacher. She knows how to ask hard questions and tells us that our answers are not right or wrong, but what we think. At first, we wouldn't answer her because we didn't want to get the wrong answer. She kept on asking us hard questions and we started to tell her what we thought. She liked that." Student 2 said, "When I write I ask myself questions like my teacher told me to do. I say who, what, when, how, and why and then I try to write about these questions in my story. Sometimes I have to go back to my word web or brainstorming sheet." Student 3 said, "Our teacher is always trying to make us think about things in another way. She said that it will make our brains hurt, so we think real hard about things when she asks us questions. She tells us to add more details in our writing and to be creative in our thinking. I write creative stories from my mind and make up things in my story that may not be true, but I get good grades on my writing. My teacher told me that I was a creative thinker. I smiled and she smiled back."

CHAPTER FIVE

DISCUSSION, SUMMARY, AND RECOMMENDATIONS

Discussion of Findings

Critical thinking is synonymous with analytical reasoning, synthesis, problem-solving, or higher mental processes (Scriven & Paul, 1992). Since critical thinking is hard to learn, students need continual opportunities to practice. Students can practice finding assumptions in textbook chapters or newspaper articles. When students encounter opposing views on complex family and social issues, they can practice expanding the two views to multiple perspectives to avoid labeling one perspective right and the other wrong. Students can examine the evidence and argumentative progression in relevant editorials. They can write five-minute papers practicing some of the skills in writing. Finally, they can write weekly learning journals to document their own learning (Kienzler & Smith, 2003).

Discussion of Findings

Research Question One: Were there differences in teachers' opinions and perceptions regarding the impact of America's Choice Program on fifth grade students' critical thinking and writing skills?

An analysis of the teacher survey on teachers' opinions about the impact of America's Choice program on fifth grade students' critical thinking and writing skills revealed that the majority of the teachers believed that students have good ability to write with clarity, use correct grammar, use correct punctuation, and the ability to develop a writing style. Further, these teachers agreed that fifth grade students had the ability to transmit information and knowledge effectively, the ability to understand what they read, and the ability to move from instructions and concepts to execution of projects, and the ability to use general concepts in the content areas.

One hundred percent of the teachers reported that students have good ability to use general concepts in the content areas and the ability to use appropriate vocabulary during writing in the content areas. The majority of the teachers felt that fifth grade students had good critical thinking skills. The majority of the teachers agreed that the America's Choice was effective because it benefited fifth grade students' writing skills and their critical thinking skills.

The majority of the teachers believed that the America's Choice program was efficient in providing staff development for teachers. Overall, teachers agreed that the America's Choice program was effective and benefited fifth graders' critical thinking and writing skills.

Research Question Two: Were there differences in teachers' opinions regarding 5th grade students' critical thinking skills as a result of their participation in the America's Choice program?

When asked if teachers initially interested in the America's Choice curriculum, the majority of teachers reported that they had no initial interest in the program and the majority of teachers were involved in a training program to teach the America's Choice curriculum. One hundred percent of the teachers were trained in the America's Choice program by the Literacy Coach. The majority of the teachers felt that the students whom they taught were experiencing difficulty in writing. However, one-third of the teachers reported that the students whom they taught were not experiencing difficulty in writing.

The majority of teachers reported that their students were not knowledgeable about how to think critically while slightly more than one-third stated that their students were knowledgeable about how to think critically. Before teachers were introduced to the America's Choice program, the majority reported that they challenged their students to be critical thinkers anyway. Teachers were equally divided in their opinions about whether or not the America's Choice curriculum had increased their students' critical thinking ability.

Overall, teachers and students believed that the America's Choice program was beneficial to teaching critical thinking. Students can develop confidence in reasoning, develop intellectual courage, think independently, read critically, and generate or assess solutions.

Research Question Three: Were there differences in 5th grade students' opinions regarding their writing skills as a result of their participation in the America's Choice program?

Focus Group 1: America's Choice participants responded positively to the program components. Students seem to enjoy writing, but what they wrote about depended on what the topic was. Others wrote only when they were assigned a topic in order to share their ideas. Students generally felt that America's Choice program has improved their writing ability. Students reported that they used brainstorming to help them organize their writing before they started to write.

The opening meeting is when teachers present a new assignment or review a writing assignment. Students felt that the opening meeting assisted them with their writing. Students seemed to enjoy writing poetry and having poems read to them. Students had an opportunity to edit and revise their writing during the opening session. Students complete their tasks during the work session as they improve on their writing skills by adding more details to a story during teacher conferencing.

When music is played, students seemed to enjoy listening while writing. Students felt that music was not a distraction because they look forward to hearing it and they were used to listening to the music. Two students stated that they listened to different types of music at home when they completed their homework assignments. In the Author's Chair, students share their stories with each other as they listen to other children read their stories.

Students reported that the Word Web was beneficial before writing their stories. The Word Web helps students to organize their thoughts and students provide more information for their stories before writing. Students select details from their stories to use in the Word Web. Students stated that they should write because that is what good writers do. Students also learned that writing is a process that requires certain steps to complete it.

Students reported that America's Choice program has been helpful when they had to collect information and decide on what information was needed for their writing. Students learned that they had to ask questions that caused them to answer to what, when, why, and how responses. Other students reported that they realized that the first writing draft was not their final writing draft and students had to re-write several drafts in order to edit and revise for their final draft.

Student Focus Group 2: Non-America's Choice Program who was not part of the group of students who participated in the program during 2004-2005 had similar comments as Student Focus Group 2. Since all teachers were trained using the concepts of the America's Choice program guidelines, many of these teachers were not part of the pilot study to determine if the program worked. Therefore, these teachers used some of America's Choice guidelines in the content areas of language arts, reading, and social studies.

Student Focus Group 2 also seemed to enjoy writing in all of their subjects as well as writing about their family and friends and other topics of interest. When asked if their writing has improved in their fifth grade year, all students responded that their teachers helped them to learn to write and stressed the importance of writing in the content areas as well as in their daily lives. Students learned how to use different types of sentences, punctuation marks, and correct grammar.

Students reported that they learned how to use descriptive writing, parts of speech, and different types of sentences, how to write business and friendly letters, and how to compare and contrast two different things. Students also learned that writing is important in their personal and school lives. Two students reported that during the work session, teachers have conferences with each student to discuss their writing, make revisions, and give suggestions for improving their writing. Journal writing as expository writing was practiced and students recorded daily events without having to be concerned with their spelling. Journals were viewed by teachers; however they were not graded, or edited for errors in spelling, punctuation, and grammar. Class work and formal writing of essays were revised and edited and graded.

Students in Focus Group 2 also seemed to enjoy listening to music while writing. One student stated that he/she listened to rhythm and blues while doing his/her homework at home, but he/she still enjoyed listening to Mozart. All students commented that listening to music helped to relax them and they were able to concentrate much better than in complete silence. These students also stated that listening to music motivated them to want to complete their writing. Another student felt that music relaxed him/her so much that he/she would sometimes become sleepy.

Students in Focus Group 2 responded that the Word Web was very helpful because they were able select the words needed for their stories. Two students stated that the Word Web provides ideas and helps them to write then they could always think of what to say and write. The Word Web was a story starter for these students. Students responded that they learned a lot in their writing class including learning to write legibly, neatly, and using correct spelling. Each student was able to use the dictionary and thesaurus when they needed to spell a word that was not on their Word Web. Students also stated that they learned the parts of speech and how to use adjectives to describe their writing.

Regarding critical thinking, students in Focus Group 2 reported that their teacher asked difficult questions that made them think so hard that thinking hurt their "brains." Their teacher helped their confidence by stating that there was no right or wrong answers in order for students to be unafraid to respond to the questions. Initially, students were hesitant about responding to questions with fear that they would give the incorrect answer. One student stated that the teacher was always trying to make students think about things in another way in order for them to become creative thinkers.

According to Norris and Ennis (1989, p. 1), critical thinking is "reasonable, reflective thinking that is focused on deciding what to believe and do." In a formal study of one college class (Smith & Kienzler, 2003), 18 undergraduate students provided insights into learning the critical thinking process. Half of the students were taking a required course and the other half took the course as an elective. Students were encouraged to practice applying the critical thinking process to personal, family, and social issues. The findings revealed that critical thinking is harder than most teachers and students expected (Brookfield, 1994; King, 1992).

Many students stated that critical thinking caused them to have a headache because they had to think so hard about things. Other students commented that critical thinking should take more than one course but should be over a long period of time.

Summary

Critical thinking is difficult because it requires students to work on two kinds of learning, both content and process simultaneously (Huba & Freed, 2000). In order to learn the content, students were required to discover the content of a topic from a wide variety of sources and resources.

Students encountered difficulty when they had to examine content from multiple perspectives as they were familiar with their personal opinions on a topic and not multiple opinions. The critical thinking process was simple until students had to practice using it. The critical thinking process included defining issues, clarifying terms, identifying assumptions of others, and evaluating (Smith & Kienzler, 2003).

Recommendations

Critical thinking is an important skill and topic in modern education (Schafersman, 1991). It is an assumption that teachers automatically teach critical thinking skills. The purpose of specifically teaching critical thinking is to improve the thinking of students and therefore better prepare them to succeed in the real world (Schafersman, 1991).

According to Schafersman (1991), critical thinking may be taught during lectures when questioning students in ways that require that they not only understand the material, but also can analyze it and apply it to new situations. Critical thinking can also be taught when assigning traditional reading homework and special written problem sets or questions used to enhance critical thinking. Homework may present many opportunities to encourage critical thinking. Exams and tests (essay and multiple choice questions) can be developed to promote critical thinking rather than rote memorization.

Critical thinking may be taught by lecturing, if the teacher periodically stops and asks students searching and thoughtful questions about the material and then wait for appropriate response time for students to answer (Smith & Kienzler, 2003). Students should be active and engaged in the learning process. Critical thinking is an active process and listening to lectures is a passive process. The intellectual skills of critical thinking include analysis, synthesis, reflection, and evaluation. Students should learn these skills by performing them in active intellectual participation (Smith & Kienzler, 2003).

For homework activities, teachers should promote critical thinking by providing students with basic questions to be answered before beginning a reading assignment. Teachers should require that students transform the information through paraphrasing, summarizing it, or outlining all reading assignments. As part of homework assignments, teachers should encourage students to write more because it is the best and perhaps the easiest way to improve critical thinking. Students may write short papers about topics of interest and paraphrase news articles and textbook chapters.

Research papers promote critical thinking among students by requiring that they evaluate, synthesize, and logically analyze information, and then present this information and conclusions in written form. Exams and teacher-made tests should require that students write, or at least think as indicated by short and long answer essay questions requiring students to analyze information and draw conclusions and make inferences. Students may use diagrams, graphic organizers, and descriptions comparing and contrasting the advantages and disadvantages of a particular topic.

Implications

Writing is a complex activity that should be incorporated into all content areas in the curriculum (The National Writing Project & Nagin, 2003). Understanding how to teach writing has evolved significantly over the last three decades (The National Writing Project & Nagin, 2003). Not only is writing a complex process, it is a means in inquiry and expression for all learning in all grades and disciplines. Today, more and more educators have come to understand that writing is central to academic success. Students need to write more across all content areas and schools need to expand their writing curricula to involve students in a range of writing tasks (The National Writing Project & Nagin, 2003). Students need to start writing early in their school years in order to become effective writers in their later years.

REFERENCES

Appalachia Educational Laboratory (AEL). (2005a). *About AEL*. Retrieved July 22, 2005 from http://www.ael.org

Appalachia Educational Laboratory (AEL). (2005b). *Effective questioning: Meeting the instructional needs of all children.* NCLB Information Center for Rural and Small School Districts. [Online]. Available: http://www.ael.org/nclb/opd002/

Alvino, J. (1990). A glossary of thinking skills terms. *Learning, 18,* 6-50.

Applebee, A. (1981). *Writing in the secondary schools: English and content areas.* NCTE Research Report No. 21, Urban, IL: National Council of Teachers of English.

Applebee, A., & Langer, I. (1986). *The writing report card: Writing achievement in American schools.* Princeton, NJ: Educational Testing Service, National Assessment of Educational Progress.

Applebee, A., J. Langer, & I.V.S. Mullis. (1986). *The writing report card: Writing achievement in American schools.* Princeton, NJ: Educational Testing Service, National Assessment of Educational Progress.

Applebee, A., Langer, J., Mullis, I.V.S., & Jenkins, L. (1990). *The writing report card, 1984-88: Findings from the nation's report card.* Princeton, NJ.

Atwell, N. (1998). *In the middle: New understandings about writing, reading, and learning.* Portsmouth, NH: Boynton/Cook.

Avery, C. (1993). *And with a light touch: Learning about reading, writing, and teaching with first graders.* Portsmouth, NH: Heinemann.

Beyer, B. (1983). Common sense about teaching thinking skills. *Educational Leadership, 41,* 44-49. EJ 289 719

Beyth-Marom, R., Novik, R., and Sloan, M. (1987). Enhancing children's thinking skills: An instructional model for decision-making under certainty. *Instructional Science, 16*(3), 215-231. Bloom, B. S., Egelhart, M. D., Furst, E. J., Hill, W. H., & Krathwohl, D. R. (1956). *Taxonomy of education objectives: Handbook I-cognitive domain.* New York, NY: David McKay Company, Inc.

Bomer, R. (1995). *Time for meaning: Crafting literate lives in middle and high school.* Portsmouth, NH: Heinemann.

Britton, J., Martian, N., McLeod, A., & Rosen, H. (1975). *The development of writing abilities.* London: Macmillan Education.

Brookfield, S. (1994). Tales from the dark side: A phenomenography of adult critical reflection. *International Journal of Lifelong Learning, 13,* 203-213.

Calkins, L. M., & Harwayne, S. (1991). *Living between the lines.* Portsmouth, NH: Heinemann.

Calkins, L. M. (1986). *The art of teaching writing.* Portsmouth, NH: Heinemann.

Carr, K. (1990). *How can we teach critical thinking.* (ERIC Document Reproduction Service No. ED 326 304)

Costa, A. (1985). *How can we recognize improved student thinking? Developing minds: A resource book for teaching thinking.* Alexandria, VA: Association for Supervision and Curriculum Development, 288-290.

Cotton, K. (1988). *Teaching thinking skills.* School Improvement Research Series (SIRS). Office of Educational Research and Improvement (OERI) (Document Reproduction No. RP 1002001).

Court, D. (1991, May/June). Teaching critical thinking: What do we know? *The Social Studies,* 115-119.

Daniels, L. B. (1975). What is the language of the practical? *Curriculum Theory Network, 4*(4), 237-261.

Educational Testing Services. (2005). *National Assessment of Educational Progress (NAEP).*

Eggan, P., & Kauckak, D. (1988). *Strategies for teachers: Teaching content and thinking skills.* Englewood Cliffs, New Jersey: Prentice-Hall.

Emig, J. (1977). Writing as a mode of learning. *College Composition and Communication, 28,* 122-128.

Ennis, R. (1985). A taxonomy of critical thinking disposition and abilities. *Journal of Teacher Education, 36*(3), 31-35.

Fisher, A. (2001). *Critical thinking: An introduction.* Cambridge, MA: Cambridge University Press.

Font, M., Todd, G., & Welch, B. (1996). *What is critical thinking?* Retrieved July 29, 1999 from www.iusb.edu~/msherida/tctstud.html

Fulwilder, T. (1980). Journals across the disciplines. *English Journal, 69*(9), 14-19.

Fulwilder, T., & Young, A. (2000). *Language connections: Writing and reading across the curriculum.* WAC Clearinghouse Landmark Publications in Writing Social Studies.

Gentry, J. R., & Gillet, J. W. (1993). *Teaching kids to spell.* Portsmouth, NH: Heinemann.

Georgia Department of Education. (2001). *Assessment and instructional guide for the Georgia Grade Five Writing Assessment.*

Gere, A. (1985). *Roots in the sawdust: Writing to learn across the disciplines.* Urbana, IL: National Council of Teachers of English.

Glasser, W. (1998). *Choice theory in the classroom.* New York, NY: Harper Trade.

Gough, D. (1991). *Thinking about thinking.* Alexandria, VA: National Association of Elementary School Principals. (ERIC Document Reproduction Service No. ED 327 980)

Graves, D. H. (1991). *The reading/writing teacher's companion: Build a literate classroom.* Portsmouth, NH: Heinemann.

Graves, D. H. (1994). *A fresh look at writing.* Portsmouth, NH: Heinemann.

Heller, M. (1995). *Reading-writing connections from theory to practice.* White Plains, NY: Longman.

Huba, M. E., & Freed, J. E. (2000). *Learner-centered assessment on college campuses: Shifting the focus from teaching to learning.* Boston: Allyn & Bacon.

Hudgins, B., & Edelman, S. (1986). Teaching critical thinking skills to fourth and fifth graders through teacher led small group discussions. *Journal of Educational Research, 79*(6), 333-342.

Hummel, J., & Huitt, W. (1994). What you measure is what you get. *GaASCD Newsletter: The Reporter,* 10-11.

Johnson, J., Holcombe, M., Simms, G., & Wilson, D. (1993). Writing to learn in a content area. *Clearing House, 66*(1), 155-158.

King, P. M. (1992). How do we know? Why do we believe? *Liberal Education, 78,* 2-9.

Langer, J., & Applebee, A. (1987). *How writing shapes thinking: A study of teaching and learning.* NCTE Research Report No. 22. Urbana, IL: National Council of Teachers of English.

Lochhead, J., & Clement, J. (1979). *An introduction to cognitive process instruction: Cognitive process instruction.* Philadelphia, PA: Franklin Institute Press.

Masters, T. (1991). The critical thinking workout. *Instructor, 100,* 64-68.

McQuain, M., & Smith, D. (1997). *Writing to learn and learning to write in mathematics.* Paper presented at the GTA Orientation Workshop 1997. Retrieved December 5, 1998, from http://www.rgs.vt.edu/gta/gta/WAC Math&Stat.html

Murray, D. (1996). *Write to learn.* Fort Worth, TX: Harcourt Brace.

National Center on Education and the Economy (NCEE). (2001). *America's Choice School Design and No Child Left Behind.* Retrieved July 22, 2005 from http://www.ncee.org/acsd/nclb/index.jsp

Norris, S. (1985). Synthesis of research on critical thinking. *Educational Leadership, 42*(8), 40-45. EJ 319 814.

Norris, S., & Ennis, R. (1989). *Evaluating critical thinking.* Pacific Grove, CA: Midwest Publication.

Pappas, C., Kiefer, B., & Levstik, L. (1995). *An integrated language perspective in the elementary school.* White Plains, NY: Longman.

Patrick, J. (1986). *Critical thinking in the social studies.* (ERIC Document Reproduction Service No. ED 272 432)

Paul, R. (1985). Bloom's Taxonomy and critical thinking instruction. *Educational Leadership, 42*(8), 36-39.

Paul, R. (1988). Critical thinking in the classroom. *Teaching K-8, 18,* 49-51.

Paul, R. (2005). *Helping our students develop critical thinking skills.* University of Toledo. Retrieved June 26, 2005 from http://www.h2000.utoledo.edu

Paul, R., & Elder, L. (2000). *The mini-guide to the art of asking essential questions: The foundation for critical thinking.* Retrieved July 10, 2005 from cct@criticalthinking.org.

Pearce, D. (1983). Guidelines for the use and evaluation of writing in content classrooms. *Journal of Reading 27,* 212-218

Peterson, R. (1992). *Life in a crowded place: Making a learning community.* Portsmouth, NH: Heinemann.

Presseisen, B. (1986). *Critical thinking and thinking skills: State of the art definition and practice in public schools.* Paper presented at the Annual Meeting of the American Educational Research Association, San Francisco, CA: (ERIC Document Reproduction Service No. ED 268 536)

Raths, L., Jonas, A., Rothstein, A., & Wessermann, S. (1967). *Teaching for thinking, theory and application.* Columbus, OH: Charles E. Merrill.

Ristow, R. (1988). The teaching of thinking skills: Does it improve creativity? *Gifted Child Today, 11*(2), 44-46.

Robinson, I. (1987). *A program to incorporate high-order thinking skills into teaching and learning for grades k-3.* Fort Lauderdale, FL: Nova University. (ERIC Reproduction Service No. ED 284 689)

Ross, C. (1998). Journaling across the curriculum. *Clearing House, 71*(3), 189-190.

Scriven, M., & Paul, R. (1992, November). *Critical thinking defined.* Handout given at the Critical Thinking Conference, Atlanta, GA.

Scriven, M., & Paul, R. (2004). *Defining critical thinking: The critical thinking community.* National Council for Excellence in Critical Thinking Instruction. [Online]. Available: http://www.criticalthinking.org

Selman, M. (1989). *Critical thinking, rationality and social practices.* Unpublished Doctoral Dissertation, University of British Columbia.

Schafersman, S. D. (1991, January). *An introduction to critical thinking.* [Online]. Available: http://www.freeinquiry.com/critical-thinking.html

Short, K., Harste, J., & Burke, C. (1996). *Creating classrooms for authors and inquirers.* Portsmouth, NH: Heinemann.

Smith, F. M., & Kienzler, D. (2003). The use of the critical thinking process by family and consumer sciences students. Kappa Omicron Nu FORUM, 14(2), 1-22. [Online]. Available: www.kon.org

Tanner, L. (1988). Observation – the path not taken: Dewey's model of inquiry. *Curricula Inquiry, 18*(4), 471-479.

Tchudi, S., & Huerta, M. (1983). *Teaching writing in the content areas middle school/junior high.* Washington, DC: National Education Association.

The National Writing Project & Nagin, C. (2003, Spring). *Because writing matters: Improving student writing in our schools.* Jossey-Bass.

ThinkQuest. (2005). *The 5 step writing process.* Retrieved July 22, 2005 from http://www.library.thinkquest.org

Tonjes, M. J., Wolpow, R., Zintz, M. V. (1999). *Integrated content literacy.* New York, NY: The McGraw-Hill Publishers. University of Wisconsin. (2005). *The writing process.* School of Education. Retrieved July 22, 2005 from http://cps.uwsp.edu

Volcano. (2005). *Peer editing and writing as process.* Retrieved July 22, 2005 from http://www.volcano.und.nodak.edu/msh/llc/is/pe.html

Wiggins, G. (1991). *Teaching to the authentic test. Educational Leadership, 46*(7), 41-47.

Williams, et al. (1989). *Focus on thinking: A unified conception.* Unpublished paper. University of Victoria.

Zinsser, W. (1989). *Write to learn.* Harper Collins Publisher.

APPENDIX A

Teacher Survey about Critical Thinking and Writing Skills

By completing and turning in this survey you are giving your consent for the researcher to include your responses in the data analyses. Your participation in this research is strictly voluntary, and you may choose not to participate without fear of penalty or any negative consequences. Individual responses will be treated confidentially. No individually identifiable information will be disclosed or published, and all results will be presented as aggregate, summary data. If you wish, you may request a copy of the results of this research by writing to the researcher at:

Natacha Billups
960 Highway 80 East
Dublin, GA 31027
(478) 272-8164
nbillups@nlamerica.com

You may also contact my dissertation chair at:

Dr. Lenneal Henderson
Fielding Graduate University
2112 Santa Barbara Street
Santa Barbara, CA 93105
(805) 898-2940
lhenderson@fielding.edu

Directions: Using the four-point Likert type scale, rate your responses to each question regarding your *fifth grade students' critical thinking and writing skills.*

4= Excellent   3 = Good   2 = Fair   1= Poor

1. Students have the ability to write with clarity.   4   3   2   1
2. Students have the ability to write using
    correct grammar.   4   3   2   1
3. Students have the ability to write using
    correct punctuation.   4   3   2   1
4. Students have the ability to develop a
    writing style.   4   3   2   1
5. Students have the ability to transmit
    information/knowledge effectively.   4   3   2   1
6. Students have the ability to understand
    what they read.   4   3   2   1
7. Students have the ability to move from
    instructions and concepts to execution
    of projects independently.   4   3   2   1
8. Students have the ability to use
    general concepts in content areas.   4   3   2   1
9. Students have the ability to use
    appropriate vocabulary during
    writing in the content areas.   4   3   2   1
10. Rate your students' critical thinking skills.   4   3   2   1
11. The America's Choice Program has
    benefited my students' writing skills.   4   3   2   1

12. The America's Choice Program has
    benefited my students' critical thinking skills.   4   3   2   1
13. The America's Choice Program provided
    ongoing staff development for teachers.   4   3   2   1
14. Overall, the America's Choice Program is
    beneficial to fifth graders.   4   3   2   1

COMMENTS: _____

_____

_____

_____

_____

_____

_____

_____

_____

_____

_____

APPENDIX B

Teacher Focus Group Questions

1. Were you initially interested in the America's Choice curriculum?
   a. Yes
   b. No

2. Did you go through a training to teach the America's Choice curriculum?
   a. Yes
   b. No

3. If you were trained, who trained you?
   a. Administrator
   b. Literacy Coach
   c. Colleague

4. Are the students whom you teach experiencing difficulty in writing?
   a. Yes
   b. No

5. Were the students whom you teach knowledgeable about how to think critically?
   a. Yes
   b. No

6. Before you were introduced to the America's Choice program, did you challenge your students to be critical thinkers?
   a. Yes
   b. No

7. Do you feel that the America's Choice curriculum has increased your students' critical thinking capability?
   a. Yes
   b. No

8. Do you feel that critical thinking and writing are important to elementary school children? Please explain.

   _____

   _____

   _____

   _____

   _____

9. Indicate three to five things the America's Choice has taught you about teaching writing?

   _____

   _____

   _____

   _____

   _____

10. Indicate three to five things the America's Choice has taught you about teaching critical thinking skills?

   _____

   _____

   _____

   _____

   _____

11. Do you stimulate students' thinking by requiring them to go beyond the factual recall or procedural levels, and engage in higher order thinking which involves the application, synthesis, and evaluation of knowledge? Please explain.

_____

_____

_____

_____

_____

12. How often do you ask your students cognitive memory questions (lower order) and focus on factual recall?

_____

_____

_____

_____

_____

13. How much of a challenge is it for you to engage your students in productive questions (ex: attention focus-focusing, measuring, comparison, action, problem posing and reasoning)?

_____

_____

_____

_____

_____

14. Did you challenge your students to use different types of thinking to answer questions such as critical thinking, creative thinking, convergent thinking, divergent thinking, inductive thinking, deductive thinking, closed thinking, open questions before the America's Choice? Please explain.

_____

_____

_____

_____

_____

15. How often did you engage students in activities which fostered high-level thinking before the America's Choice program?

_____

_____

_____

_____

_____

APPENDIX C

1. Did you enjoy writing before America's Choice program began? Please explain.

   _____
   _____
   _____
   _____
   _____

2. Do you feel that working with America's Choice program has improved your writing ability? Please explain.

   _____
   _____
   _____
   _____
   _____

3. Do you feel that you learned anything during the opening meeting? If so please explain?

   _____
   _____
   _____
   _____
   _____

4. What is your task during the work session?

_____

_____

_____

_____

_____

5. When you are writing in the work session, does the music (Mozart: "Strengthen the Mind") cause a distraction? Please explain.

_____

_____

_____

_____

_____

6. What takes place in the Author's Chair?

_____

_____

_____

_____

_____

7. Did you find the word web to be beneficial before writing?

_____

_____

_____

_____

_____

8. Indicate three to five things that America's Choice program has taught you about writing?

_____

_____

_____

_____

_____

9. Indicate three to five things that America's Choice has taught you about critical thinking?

_____

_____

_____

_____

_____

APPENDIX D

1. Do you enjoy writing? Please explain.

    _____

    _____

    _____

    _____

    _____

2. Do you feel that your writing has improved in your 5th grade year? Please explain.

    _____

    _____

    _____

    _____

    _____

3. Explain and/or list some of the things you learned in your writing class.

    _____

    _____

    _____

    _____

    _____

4. During your work session, what are you required to do?

_____

_____

_____

_____

_____

5. How do you feel about writing when music is being played? Does it motivate you or distract you? Please explain.

_____

_____

_____

_____

_____

6. Did you find the word web to be beneficial before writing?

_____

_____

_____

_____

_____

7. Indicate three to five things you learned in your writing class.

_____

_____

_____

_____

_____

8. Indicate three to five things your teacher has taught you about critical thinking.

   _____

   _____

   _____

   _____

   _____

APPENDIX E

Letter for Principal's Permission to Conduct Study

Principal
Elementary School
Dublin, Georgia 31027

Dear Sir:

I am writing this letter to seek permission to conduct a research study at the selected elementary school. This research will be used in writing my dissertation for the doctoral program at Fielding Graduate Institute located in Santa Barbara, California. I am requesting access to fifth grade students' composite Georgia Grade Five Writing Assessment results during 2004-2005. The length of this research project will be conducted beginning September, 2005 and ending approximately January, 2006.

The title of my dissertation is An Analysis of the Impact of the America's Choice Program on Critical Thinking and Writing Skills of Selected Fifth Grade Students. This research is intended for elementary students to be able to use questioning techniques when they are faced with academic tasks. First, all fifth grade teachers will participate in a teachers' survey regarding the impact of America's Choice program on fifth grade students' critical thinking and writing skills.

Second, the first six (6) teachers who complete and turn in their signed informed consent forms will be selected to participate in a focus group interview that will last approximately 60 minutes after school. Finally, fifth grade students' writing scores from the Georgia Grade Five Writing Assessment will be examined and analyzed to describe students' critical thinking and writing skills. This qualitative and quantitative study will be conducted and evaluated through teachers' survey data, focus group interview data, performance base writing scores data, and statistical analyses of the results.

I realize by law and board policy that I should adhere to the Family Educational Rights and Privacy Act (FERPA). I assure you that rights and privacy acts of everyone concerned will not be compromised.

I would like to thank you very much for your consideration in allow me to conduct this research. I look forward to hearing from you soon. Please sign the form below and return it to me as soon as possible.

Sincerely,

Natacha Z. Billups
Doctoral Student
Fielding Graduate University

cc: Superintendent of Schools
       Associate Superintendent of Curriculum

_____ Yes, I give permission for Natacha Z. Billups to conduct a research study at the selected elementary school. I understand that prior permission must be obtained from the school system before I can legally grant permission at this school.

Permission to conduct a research study has been granted to Ms. Natacha Z. Billups at the selected elementary school in Dublin, Georgia.

_____   _____

Please print your full name and title   Date

_____   _____

Please sign your full name and title   Date

APPENDIX F

Teacher Recruitment Letter

Dear Teachers:

As many of you are aware, I am completing my doctoral work in the school of Educational Leadership and Change at Fielding Graduate University in Santa Barbara, California. My dissertation focus is on the impact of the America's Choice program on fifth grade students' critical thinking and writing skills.

I would like to invite you to participate in this study by becoming a volunteer participant in a focus group to discuss students' and critical thinking and writing skills. This focus group will take place after school in the Gold Room for approximately 60 minutes. The focus group interview will be audio-taped. Neither your name nor identity will be used in this study. Each teacher will have a pseudonym to protect your identity and provide your comments with complete confidentiality. The principal will not have access to the transcription and the audio-tapes.

If you would like to participate in this study, please respond to this letter. I will send you a consent form to help you understand your rights in this study. Due to the scope of this study, I will only accept six (6) people for the focus group. The first six teachers to positively respond to this recruitment letter will be accepted. I will maintain other names in order of receipt. If one of the first six respondents withdraws for some reason, I will contact you to take their place.

You should be aware that there are minimal risks associated with this study. The exchange of information concerning the issue of critical thinking and writing may provide a better understanding of the benefits of higher order thinking skills and writing. This can lead to a great sense of empowerment. Further, there may be times during the focus group process that you may experience a myriad of emotions that may cause feelings of frustration, happiness or sadness.

I look forward to your participation in this research study.

Sincerely,

Natacha Z. Billups
Doctoral Student
Fielding Graduate University

APPENDIX G

Informed Consent Letter for Teachers

Dear Fifth Grade Teachers:

My name is Natacha Z. Billups and I am a doctoral student in the school of Educational Leadership and Change at Fielding Graduate University, Santa Barbara, California. I am also a fifth grade teacher in Laurens County Public School. As a teacher, I have observed the need for students to use higher order thinking skills. Therefore, I am conducting a study to analyze teachers' opinions regarding the impact of the America's Choice program components on selected fifth grade students' critical thinking and writing skills. Because these students are either in your classes or are your children, your experiences and opinions are important to this study.

I invite you to participate in this study by participating in a teachers' survey to express your opinions about the impact of the America's Choice program on fifth grade students' critical thinking and writing skills. The teachers' survey will take place after school in the Gold Room for approximately 30 minutes. You will be notified of the date and time at a later time. Neither your name nor identity will be used in this study. Each survey will be numbered for tracking purposes only during data input. The principal will not have access to the teachers' surveys. The results will be analyzed in the final report of this study.

You are encouraged to refuse to answer any question(s) posed to you. There is no penalty for not participating in this study. If you choose to participate, you may withdraw from this study at any time either during or after your participation, by contacting me, without negative consequences.

Should you withdraw, your data will be eliminated from the study and will be destroyed. If you participate in the questionnaire and then choose to withdraw, every effort will be made to delete your initial data.

In addition, I am requesting your participation in a teacher focus group to discuss the impact of America's Choice program on fifth grade students' critical thinking and writing skills. You may be asked to provide a pseudonym; that is your real name will never be used. The information you provide will remain confidential. The data will be secured in a locked file cabinet, to which only the researcher has access to the key. All data will be destroyed after a period of three years. The results of this will be used in my dissertation and possibly published in professional publications.

You should be aware that there are minimal risks associated with this study such as the process of the exchange of information concerning the impact of the America's Choice program on fifth grade students' critical thinking and writing skills. This can lead to a great sense of empowerment. Further, there may be times during the questionnaire that you may experience a myriad of emotions that may cause feelings of frustration, happiness, or sadness.

Should you at any time feel discomfort, or have any questions regarding this study, please contact me at:

960 Highway 80 East
Dublin, GA 31027
nbillups@nlamerica.com

You may also contact my dissertation chair, Dr. Lenneal Henderson at:

Fielding Graduate University
2112 Santa Barbara Street
Santa Barbara, CA 93105
(805) 898-2940
lhenderson@fielding.edu

If you consent to participate in this study, please sign this letter and return it in the self-addressed envelope provided. Please print, sign, and date the bottom of both copies of this letter. Included are two copies of this consent form, please sign one and return it in the self-addressed stamped envelope included in this mailing. Please keep the other copy for yourself. If you have any questions about any part of this study or your involvement, please tell the researcher before signing this form.

There is no monetary payment for participating in this study.

You may request a copy of the summary of the final results by completing the attached form. The Institutional Review Board of Fielding Graduate University retains access to signed informed consent forms.

_____Yes, I want to participate in this study. I understand that my consent ends at the conclusion of this study.

_____No, I do not want to participate in this study.

Print Name: _____

Signature: _____ Date: _____

Respectfully,

Natacha Z. Billups
Doctoral Student
Fielding Graduate University

APPENDIX H

Assent Letter for Fifth Grade Students

Dear Fifth Grade Student:

My name is Ms. Natacha Z. Billups. I am also in school just like you. I am trying to find ways to help our school improve or get better to serve you in your educational needs. If you would like to help improve our school, would you be willing to take part in a study that I am doing? I want you to participate in a small group of three students. I will ask you some questions and I want you to answer. There is no right or wrong answer. I want to know what you think about the America's Choice program.

The risks to you for being in the study are low. They include feeling, sad, happy, or angry. You can benefit from this study when your teachers better understand your writing styles. The information gathered will assist teachers in helping you become a better thinker and writer.

If you would like to help improve our school, please indicate your choice to take part or not to take part in this study. Your name will not be written or recorded anywhere in this study.

 Yes, I would like to take part.
 No, I would not like to take part.

Should you at any time feel discomfort, and should you have any questions regarding this study, please contact me at:

Natacha Z. Billups
708 Stewart Ave.
Dublin, GA 30135
(478) 272-8164
nbillups@nlamerica.com

You may also contact my dissertation chair, Dr. Lenneal Henderson at: Fielding Graduate University at 211 Santa Barbara Street.

Santa Barbara, CA 93105
(805) 898-2940
ljhenderson@fielding.edu

Please sign your name below:

_____
Your Signature   Date

_____
Researcher's Signature   Date

Sincerely,

Ms. Natacha Z. Billups
Doctoral Student
Fielding Graduate University

APPENDIX I

Informed Consent Letter for Parents

Dear Parents,

My name is Natacha Z. Billups and I am a doctoral student in the school of Educational Leadership and Change at Fielding Graduate University, Santa Barbara, California. I am also a fifth grade teacher in the selected school. As a teacher I have observed the need for students to use higher order thinking skills. Therefore, I am conducting a study to determine the roots of these challenges. Because these students are your children, your experiences and opinions are important to the study.

I would appreciate your consent for your child to participate in a focus group with two other students to determine if the America's Choice program has any impact on their critical thinking and writing skills. There is no penalty for not letting your child participate in this study. If you choose for your child to participate, you may withdraw from this study at any time either during or after your participation, by contacting me, without negative consequences.

The information you provide about your child will remain confidential. The data will be secured in a locked file cabinet, to which only the researcher has access to the key. All data will be shredded after a period of three years. The results of this will be used in my dissertation and possibly published in professional publications.

You should be aware that there are minimal risks associated with this study. The process of using your child's comments in a group may lead feelings of sadness. Your child's name will not be used to identify your child.

Should you have any questions regarding this study, please contact me at:

960 Highway 80 East
Dublin, GA 31027
nbillups@nlamerica.com

You may also contact my dissertation chair, Dr. Lenneal Henderson at:

Fielding Graduate University
2112 Santa Barbara Street
Santa Barbara, CA 93105
(805) 898-2940
lhenderson@fielding.edu

If you consent to participate in this study, please sign this letter and return it in the self-addressed stamped envelope provided. Please print, sign, and date the bottom of both copies of this letter. Included are two copies of this consent form, please sign one and return it in the self-addressed stamped envelope included in this mailing. Please keep the other copy for yourself. If you have any questions about any part of this study or your involvement, please tell the researcher before signing this form.

There is no monetary payment for participating in this study.

You may request a copy of the summary of the final results by completing the attached form. The Institutional Review Board of Fielding Graduate University retains access to signed informed consent forms.

_____Yes, I am granting permission for my child to participate in a focus group. I have read and understand the contents of this letter. I also understand that my consent ends at the conclusion of this study.

_____No, I do not want my child to participate in this study.

Print Child's Name: _____

Parent's Signature: _____Date: _____

Respectfully,

Natacha Z. Billups

Doctoral Student

Fielding Graduate University

****

_____   Yes, I would like a copy of the final results from this study.

Name: _____
               First   Last

Address: _____

_____

Phone: _____

Email: _____

Once again, I thank you for your participation.

Natacha Z. Billups

Doctoral Student

Fielding Graduate University